The Day and the Dweller
A Study of the Emerald Tablets

Jonathan Thompson

Edited by Antonio Garcia

Mwanaka Media and Publishing Pvt Ltd,
Chitungwiza Zimbabwe
*

Creativity, Wisdom and Beauty

Publisher: Mmap
Mwanaka Media and Publishing Pvt Ltd
24 Svosve Road, Zengeza 1
Chitungwiza Zimbabwe
mwanaka@yahoo.com
www.africanbookscollective.com/publishers/mwanaka-media-and-publishing
https://facebook.com/MwanakaMediaAndPublishing/

Distributed in and outside N. America by African Books Collective
orders@africanbookscollective.com
www.africanbookscollective.com

ISBN: 978-1-77929-593-4
EAN: 9781779295934

© Jonathan Thompson 2020

All rights reserved.
No part of this book may be reproduced or transmitted in any form or by any means, mechanical or electronic, including photocopying and recording, or be stored in any information storage or retrieval system, without written permission from the publisher

DISCLAIMER
All views expressed in this publication are those of the author and do not necessarily reflect the views of *Mmap*.

Mwanaka Media and Publishing Editorial Board:

Publisher/ Editor-in-Chief: Tendai Rinos Mwanaka
mwanaka13@gmail.com
East Africa and Swahili Literature: Dr Wanjohi wa Makokha
makokha.justus@ku.ac.ke
East Africa English Literature: Andrew Nyongesa (PhD student)
nyongesa55.andrew@gmail.com
East Africa and Children Literature: Richard Mbuthia
ritchmbuthia@gmail.com
Legal Studies and Zimbabwean Literature: Jabulani Mzinyathi
jabumzi@gmail.com
Economics, Development, Environment and Zimbabwean Literature: Dr Ushehwedu Kufakurinani ushehwedu@gmail.com
History, Politics, International relations and South African Literature: Antonio Garcia antoniogarcia81@yahoo.com
North African and Arabic Literature: Fethi Sassi sassifathi62@yahoo.fr
Gender and South African Literature: Abigail George
abigailgeorge79@gmail.com
Francophone and South West African Literature: Nsah Mala
nsahmala@gmail.com
West Africa Literature: Macpherson Okpara
chiefmacphersoncritic@gmail.com
Media studies and South African Literature: Mikateko Mbambo
me.mbambo@gmail.com
Portuguese and West Africa Literature: Daniel da Purificação
danieljose26@yahoo.com.br

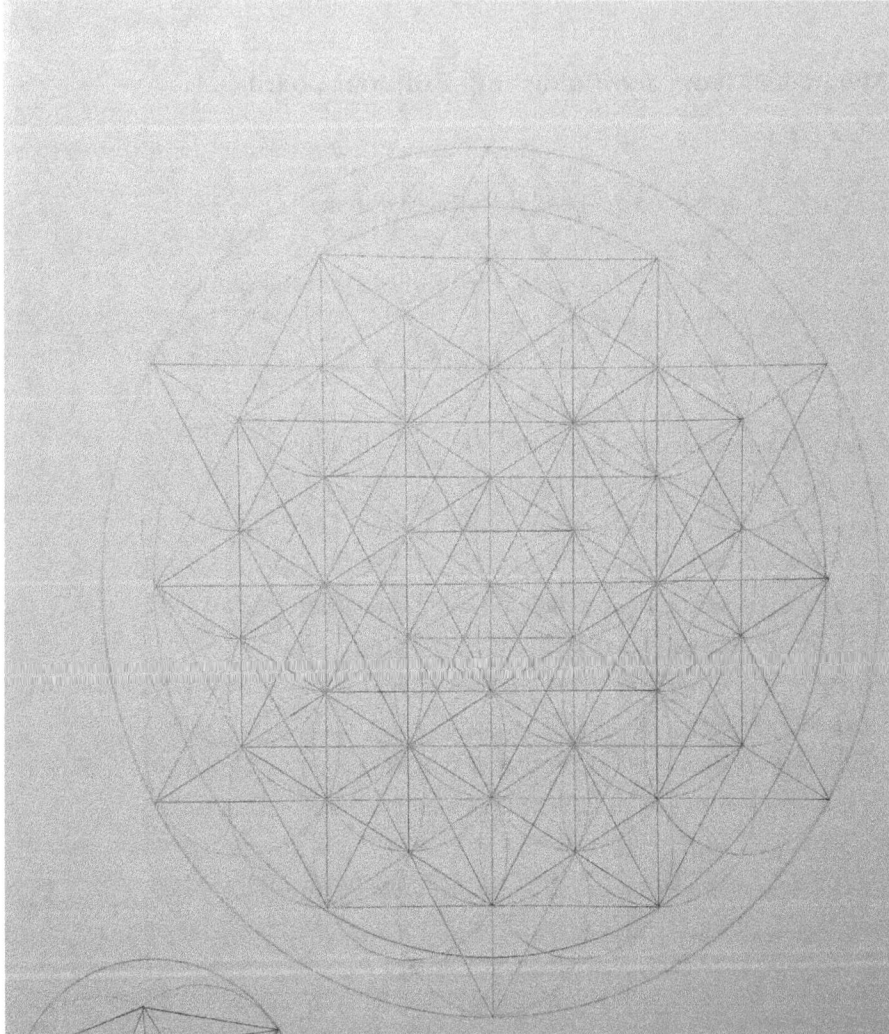

"Hear ye now of one who is liberated, free from the bondage of life into light. Knowing the source of all worlds shall be open. Aye, even the gates of Arulu shall not be barred. Yet heed, O man who would'st enter heaven, If ye be not worthy better to fall into the fire" The Emerald Tablets

TABLE OF CONTENTS

Preface..vi

Chapter 1: Moments that make you question...........................2

Chapter 2: An inward understanding..9

Chapter 3: The law...37

Chapter 4: Facing the truth..76

Chapter 5: Beyond Human..94

Chapter 6: A new look at the old way...................................111

Chapter 7: The power of self-exposure.................................125

Chapter 8: The Great Pyramid...137

Chapter 9: What's your next step?..158

Mmap Nonfiction and Academic series................................203

Preface

It is said that the tablets are formed from a substance created through alchemical transmutation rendering them imperishable, resistant to all elements and substances. In effect their atomic and cellular structure is fixed. As such they violate the laws of ionization and thus our laws of physics. They are also referred to as the Smaragdine Table, Tabula Smaragdina, or more commonly simply the Emerald Tablet, this elusive object is said to be one or even a series of rectangular green plaques.

Upon the tablets are engraved characters in the ancient Atlantean language that spell out all manner of magical knowledge, in particular having to do with alchemy and the transmutation of matter from one form to another. The characters which respond to attuned thought waves, release an associated mental vibration in the mind of the reader. The wisdom contained therein is the foundation of the ancient mysteries. It is claimed that the one who reads it with an open mind, shall increase their wisdom by a hundred-fold.

Read and the vibration found therein will awaken a response in your soul. The proof we seek that forever separates what we know and what we think we know lay in the words you will read. The removal of the dogmatic indoctrination and the misperceptions it has created. A proof of love that lay sleeping behind the eyes waiting to be woken by those who senses there is more to this great world than what we have been taught. An inner world of light and of love. To know, one must apply. Read and think. Read and feel. Read and see. Read and Know. Convert the knowledge to wisdom and you will be free. In the silence of the material senses lies the key to the unveiling of wisdom. "He who talks does not know, he who knows does not talk"

Unlocking the Divine self has for millennia been more of a myth than a reality as so many has sort to find the gift of eternal life. Some claim that eternal life only exists in the fiction created by the mind. I would disagree. I share in part through these writings a journey into the past and sometimes mythical unknown to remember the long forgotten.

Within reason, we all have the gift of free will, we decide our path. This is the path I chose...

The octahedron drawn on the strange angles within the alpha cubex representing the inner and outer self as one. These images are a direct interpretation from the codex with the Divine Self unlocked only when the all ones become one. They are keys. Spend time with them. They are more powerful than you know.

Chapter 1

Moments that make you question

I didn't think there was any point going down that dark road. The search was over, there was nothing left to look for, there was nothing worth holding on to anymore. I had fallen many times but never like this. "Where are you!!?" I cried bitterly as the next brutal blow knocked me down harder. My heart was broken. There was so little fight left in me. It was a hopeless feeling, losing control, I didn't care anymore.

The pain had become unbearable living with so many questions that could never be answered, too many words that were said and yet remained forever unsaid. I was alone, trying to hold onto the last remaining memories that time had blown away with the unread letters and the burning pieces of my broken self. "It always ended this way. Why does it always end this way!!?" What did it matter, just another new beginning and another miserable beginning's end.

I was tired, worn away by the brutal war that blacked out the years of endless sorrows. I didn't know how to put myself back together anymore. I didn't even care whether I may have been having a heart attack. I should've just died, I wasn't supposed to live this long but unfortunately I was still here. So were these tears, keeping me warm in this insanity. I knew this pain but it has never knocked me down this hard. I didn't know how to get up. A part of me didn't want to get up. I didn't know how to admit to myself that I was not in control of what had happened. I thought I knew myself but this has never happened before. I wasn't okay, I had known this for most of my life. The years had caught up with me. This nightmare of being awake was as bad as the nightmares that followed me into my sleep. The angels and demons and the insidious agony, invisible and deadly. My wounds never showed on my body and yet bled deeper the cavern of emptiness. My attempts to conceal it daily had only increased the burden but the absence of the will to live was not sufficient to make me want to die. A part of me was afraid but I knew it was time I too take a look at the past and find some meaning to this misery.

I took time off, I needed time but even my peaceful home was filled with the unmistakable irritation of the emptiness success brings. Although this could be easily avoided with the ignorance that distraction brings. I knew my discomfort and the breakdown was linked but I was so sedated by the extremes of my lifestyle it never surfaced this aggressively before. I took a moment to consider what happened because I needed to understand. Even though I was facing certain defeat I had to know what happened and what it meant.

I turned to any research material I could find trying to make sense of the human mind's connection to its biology. It came with boundaries and censorship. All the medical advice I found only considered the physical symptoms and not the emotional connection. My thoughts kept taking me inward? A strange place I was not interested in exploring. I am not an introspective person.

I had been hurt. Most of me was shutdown, with only the scars left from years of self-imposed torture. I spent more time maintaining my defenses than my well-being. My emotions had been relegated to the shadows and were rarely the driving force of my conscious decision making. Instead objectives replaced emotions. I was cold, precise, arrogant, ignorant and in control, or so I thought.

My decision making was organized by proper planning thus preventing poor performances, or so goes the adage. I based my understanding of all things through constructing a hypothesis, doing good research to support it. Finding independent sources that verifies or relays a similar consensus. Test to confirm and analyze accordingly. Communicate results and refine where required even if I had to start over. This was the trusted scientific approach.

When I spoke to people it often left me with more questions than answers. Most were nursing their own pre-existing conditions no different from me. No one ever spoke at any real depth, yet they believed in their opinion which at times was untested, unvalidated and despite this, packaged as truth. I was a product of lies. This type of deceptive formation made me suspicious and apprehensive.

"Was there nothing else, no easier way?" My research wasn't getting me anywhere, a combination of a lack of symmetrical connection, limited findings and capitalist agendas are not the best mechanisms for researching the surfacing of emotions. I was missing something but what? Maybe I wasn't looking in the right place. In truth I wasn't looking hard enough because a part of me wanted to forget and move on, move back to the safety of old routines.

I forced myself to confront my past. Something inside of me knew there was more. I was compelled to dig deeper. I had always been interested in alternative theories of the world and the philosophies of natural healing because it seemed to make more sense than the modern practices with which I had many failed experiences. I had to consider all avenues. It took months researching, investigating and testing theories. I linked one piece to another putting it all together across every field, not just medicine and healing but every aspect that related to the human. Modern sources felt corrupt or lacking in something I could not quite identify, so I went as far back as I could to ancient historical sources.

It was this thought principle that aligned me with the old teachings. The way of the ancients resonated with me. I wasn't sure why exactly but working through the old writings and viewing the ancient structures showed a deeper comprehension of the power and potential of the self. These teachings today are only kept alive through tribal cultures. Modern religions do not acknowledge these older traditions referring to them as works of mysticism. Certain ancient practices do seem very far removed from what is currently acceptable such as eating your enemy's heart or bathing in blood to gain super human strength or eternal life. With great irony I found connections between modern religions and older tribal cultures.

The present norm is to judge and discard too easily. I was equally guilty of judging too easily and too harshly but this had to change somehow. The ancients spoke of an inward journey. They spoke of a balance with oneself and nature which I didn't fully understand. What I did understand was that a journey inward would require honesty I was not in good shape and I needed to take care of myself. I didn't mind admitting this in relation to my physical health but my emotional health was a different matter. There was a part of me that knew what I needed, what I wanted, what I would and wouldn't do. I thought I knew the difference between right and wrong. I was arrogantly aware of my condition but I was oblivious to the true state of the dweller within.

What I did know is the tears and that night had surely opened and exposed something deeper than just my broken heart. Even though just for a moment it gave me a glimpse into the forgotten. The pain I buried was rotting away inside. This dissolved my arrogant pride. When it surfaced that night, I felt a small part of what was really inside. My self-medicating ways had turned my home into a drug den. The pain had become so intense that I was struggling to maintain my fragile balance between order and madness. I knew my addictions were out of control. A part of me was looking for the escape that death brings. "It is not seen as insane when a fighter, under an attack that will inevitably lead to his death, chooses to take his own life first. In fact, this act has been encouraged for centuries, and is accepted even now as honorable. How is it any different when you are under attack by your own mind?"

For me drugs and alcohol is more controllable than other addictions and conditions such as eating disorders. We live in a world where make-up, compulsive shopping, cell phones, laziness, late sleeping, making excuses are equal addictions that mask inner sadness. Just because we may not recognize these, and they are not illegal doesn't mean they are not equally problematic. Although, this was a defensive response and though it may be valid it was an excuse that I had used many times over to justify my choices. I had to make some changes.

Bad history

I was born with health issues like a defective model which came off the assembly line, my parents should have taken me back for repairs before the warranty ran out. I was constantly battling asthma, hay fever, sinus, the flu, fever, bronchitis and other chest related issues. These required several operations in my younger years yet they could never mend the post nasal drip those operations were meant to cure. I was fed medication which at times included more than 12 pills 3 times a day. This was normal for me. I get ill, go to the doctor, they give me enough medication and eventually I recover. This is how I lived my life, I had never thought to question it any further.

As I child, photos shows me smiling and happy yet my earliest living memory was of frantic running. I was just a boy but I remember what panic and pain felt like. My smile became the mask. There was a face beneath that mask, but it wasn't me either. When I was very young I ran away from home. I had determined that if they were chasing me my parents couldn't argue with each other. I was young enough to understand this and yet not old enough to go to school. As with many children I became a student of manipulation.

Witnessing my parent's failed attempts to communicate, each one convinced the other was wrong and never finding a peaceful lasting solution had a lasting impact on me. Neither willing to right the wrongs instead staying together in what they had determined was happiness. I saw the cruel power of forgiveness. This was the power they held over each other. To withhold or bestow it was a power, perhaps often used for the wrong reasons. Maybe none of it was about control? Maybe it was all about control? Maybe it wasn't about who could own who but who can do what to whom and get away with it. I was too young to know. This was the life I remembered, only the negative, all the good dissolved away.

These memories in part had resurfaced after that night. I've struggled with poor memory most of my life so this must have mattered to me. Other memories returned too that had been long lost and through that difficult experience I felt just a little better. I've never known any real peace long enough to describe it and compare to something else.

I didn't know that once triggered we shut down and retreat resetting if required and dumping the memory. I learnt this in my studies. This shutdown space was the way in but it was dark there. Regardless it was the only clue I had. I didn't know if I was strong enough to be present with more of the horror of old but this was where I had to go, perhaps I could find some answers, some closure, anything to stop the bleeding. I was afraid, lost in this wilderness of the old. I knew there were reasons why I forgot my history. I was always influenced by it and whilst it didn't automatically determine what I became I could see myself growing up in the image of the old way even though I denied it. I did not want to admit this because I fought for so long to be more than the sum of those limitations and yet I was bound equally fighting an enemy I didn't understand.

It was my responsibility to free myself but I had tried so many times before. I was cursed with not being able to give up but if I could release myself from the repeating patterns that had crippled my reason and blackened my heart maybe then I could rest for a while. I was in need of rest. These days I struggled to keep my eyes open yet I never slept either, always another night and the burden of the impending morning.

I tried once more speaking to as many people who would listen and listened to as many who would speak. I had to make sense of it all but it felt impossible. Something was out of place because too often conversations relating to emotions were shut down immediately, people changed the subject or obvious lies were sold as good advice. Perhaps I was talking to the wrong people but I don't think I was. Were people just terrified children looking for the happy ending to this story of life that contained more darkness than light and the closer to the end they came the more terrified they became that there would be no light? It was feeling that way. I didn't expect this and after many failed attempts I returned to the ancient teachings. Whilst some were deeply coded I found myself able to read a little deeper between the lines and could relate to it. I had never ascribed to any form of spiritual or metaphysical teachings and I myself was not in any way interested in the spiritual or metaphysical. However, from an engineering perspective I could draw on the symmetry. I could see the essence of the same or similar message repeating veiled in symbols and I slowly began to make sense of what at first was senseless.

Chapter 2

An inward understanding

Through my research I had determined that we have only ever tuned into the default radio station which we call life and are unaware that more stations exist. We may know this as our comfort zones (At least it is the easiest way to create a relatable understanding). Consider if you will, that our radios or minds had several stations with different frequencies like the different colors of light, cycling through rhythmic time always oscillating in a continuous loop not the linear time we are familiar with. *"Time and space are moving in circles. Know ye their law, and ye too, shall be free."*

This movement of energy can be related to and is known by many names, the Chakras, Sephiroth, Chi etc. they are the energy meridians of the body. *"One within the other, yet separate in Law"* According to my research our true purpose is the pursuit of the awakening of these energies and the greater purpose that lies beyond. Not the perceived awakening way through sexual expressive energy *though it has its purposes via temporary discharge.* Our energies are cut off through our own historical circumstance and absence of awareness, the key energy being that of the heart where all of the universes secrets lay, also all the grief of life's heartaches.

I found this from the old texts *"That which Goethe into the storehouse must come forth and that which is thine must be shared with a friend."* I had a lot stored inside, but this felt like it had a deeper meaning. The texts also said the gateway to the true heart is secret. It has always been protected and mirrored as if it didn't exist and in truth for me it didn't but knowing this fact helped me make some sense of what happened that evening. There was a lot that needed re-consideration and re-evaluation. If life wasn't a random collection of events then what was it? What was I not seeing? I always read that we attract to us what we are, this sounded strange as opposites attracted surely? I felt to a degree that I was cast into a role for a play that I didn't know about. Thus, I began to consider the company I kept, who were the people I shared the stage with. All my relationships would need re-assessment because for all of my life I was bound by a deep sense of ignorant loyalty. I had to realize that the insults and teachings may not resemble each other in any way yet they must have been part of the same purpose or were connected in some way. I was confused because of my contradictory perception of the way we have been taught that the world works vs the ancients understanding of it. They spoke of myself as the observer? Accompanied by the dweller? What did this all mean? Who's the dweller? At this point my truth felt a lot like another's lie and I never enjoyed being lied to. Trying to separate it all was impossibly hard, but I still had one clue. I knew my breakdown brought a positive result, so I could repeat and continue to release because I had more things inside that were out of place.

I needed time to fully assess. I knew myself better than anyone, but I was struggling here. How would a stranger help me yet every stranger, friend and enemy apparently was me? Getting access to the heart and mind and passing my own defenses would be no easy task but I wasn't willing to place my wellbeing in the hands of another, as then surely I would be lost forever. I had to stop saying "I can't" and instead I

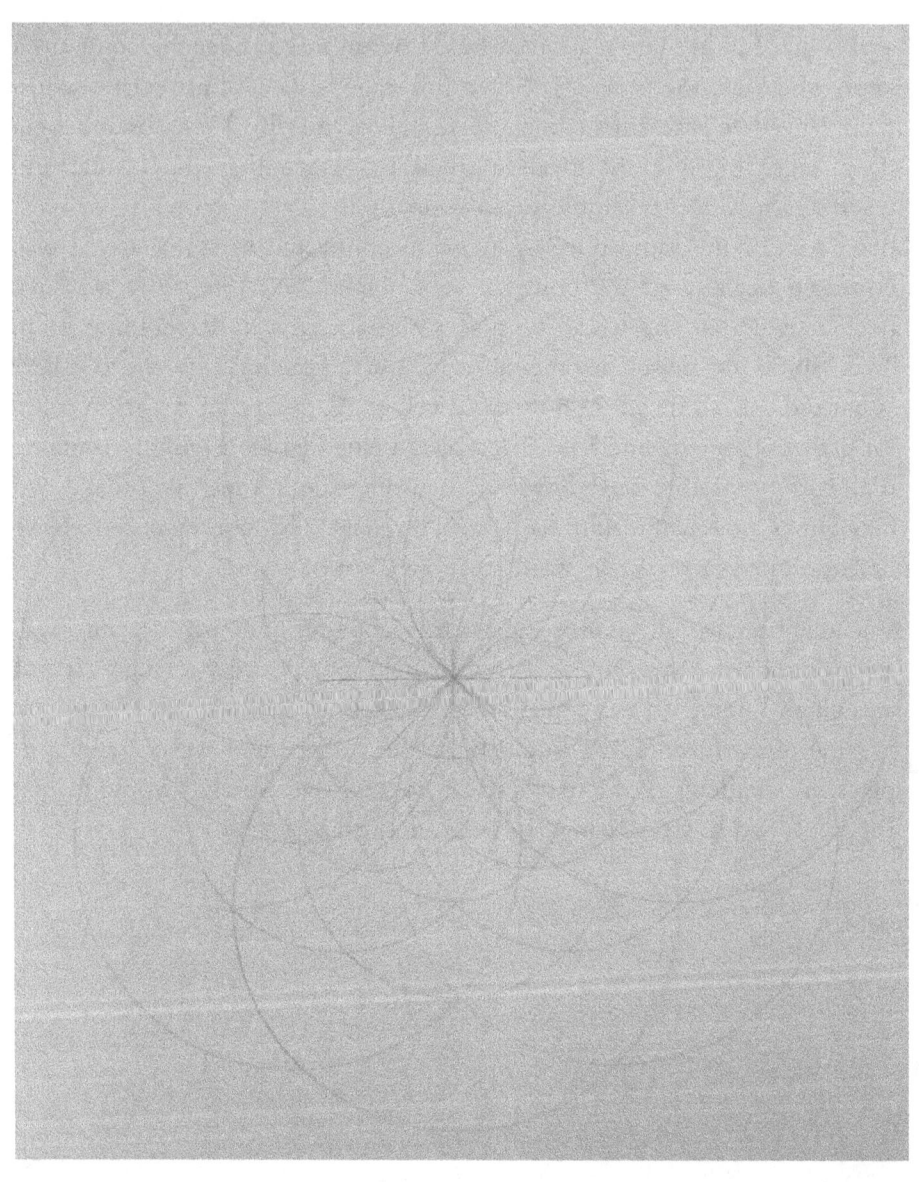

This is a four by two way expanding fractal of the heart, the geometry is the curved blue print for the great pyramid and the fractal expansion of the earth and the moon. This is the first step to finding the deep buried truth within. *See the spirals, if the*

pyramids had a technical drawing it would start off looking like this. "Built I the great pyramid patterned after the pyramid of earth force" Thoth Emerald Tablets

started saying "I won't". That became my first Master Reference. It wasn't easy doing this in a world of excuses and finger pointing. I didn't like being wrong and I had a tendency to defend my position. Many times I'd become blinded and lost sight of right and wrong.

Whilst thinking about it all my mind wandered as a thought appeared, "You know the way. You know where it ends each time. Start there. How would your life be different if you stopped worrying about things you can't control and started focusing on the things you can? Let today be the day you free yourself from fruitless worry and act on the things you can change. Should you choose this path, should you have the will I will show you the way."

A peace had come over me in the stillness which was impossible to ignore. It felt like everything was going to be okay and I could breathe. I knew this feeling for in all my ages it is the one thing I had always searched for in another. Someone who would care enough not to lie to me. It was so hard through the years watching people lie to me. I was a good person - one who would've done anything for anyone. It hurts really bad being cheated on that way, another piece of me was taken with every forgiveness that promised it would never happen again but it always did.

One of the worst things about trusting someone is really believing that everything they ever told you was the truth. It fractured me. Raised a hatred in the spirit. I had lost my respect for most women, I had no respect for almost anyone and in the end, I did terrible things. I became the cheater and many suffered in this sadistic cycle of madness. Worst of all was knowing that I let her down, I didn't know the truth but I walked away, I abandoned her because it was easier than taking responsibility for what I had done. Now I wait in the winds as the years pass hoping one day I will know the truth, even then I think it would be too late. I was wrong. All I could say was that I was sorry. "I am so sorry for letting you down."

I lost myself in that moment staying present just enough. The voice left me powerless to contain myself and what felt like a lifetime of shame inside. "My shattered heart." I have stood guard but I am tired and I cannot fight anymore. I am broken and lost in these angles of time. All I've known is pain. All I feel is desperation. I don't know how to ask for help and when I do no one listens. No matter how loud I've cried I can't stop or change what is happening. No matter what I do, the pain remains. I have betrayed myself and yet betrayal is too simple a word to describe this overwhelming feeling, the loneliness and the isolation. I've tried growing stronger, I have done as I was told with the utmost compliance but I have forgotten everything I've ever wanted. This pain still lurks. I fear I have made some bad choices you will not approve of and I'm so very sorry. I don't know how to make things right.

The voice said with great calm... *"You do not know how to forgive yourself, you do not believe that there is forgiveness for what you have done. It is a choice you make, forgive yourself and you will be free but you can only know this after you do because you are blind here, take my hand and let me show you the way. This is the other side of a life you know as death. It is your first time beyond the dark forest. You'll not stay here but know that here exists. Remember this feeling, hold onto it and it will guide your way back here".*

It was the first time in my life I had experienced something like this. These were my thoughts but it didn't feel like my words. I didn't know who this voice was and didn't understand what was going on but I knew the feeling and that was enough. I had never felt secure enough to let go this way and I didn't know that these words were inside of me. That day something changed. I didn't know exactly what but I was not the same after.

Hearts are fragile, mine broke and was never repaired. It never healed through the years of expectation, disappointment, abandonment and rejection. No one magically becomes an adult the day they turn eighteen. Some people grow up sooner, many grow up later. Some never really do. I grew up fast being a barrier between my parents. Hope faded with time's brutal beating, slowly starving me of the life-giving light of love until stonewalled I lost myself between the fragments of despair that had grown greater through the years.

I felt myself shutting down with anger not very long after the comfort of letting go. I didn't want to look deeper. There was no need to look deeper. Tears and weakness walk hand in hand. I was angry and these words were in me too. This strength more real, no different from any brave face earned through the years of my ignorance. I did not want to break the fragile peace inside afraid of allowing anyone to see, afraid of hoping again. My defenses had taken over but for the first time I could see the separation within. The calming voice faded away and I, the cold reminder of old remained. I had forgotten that anybody can become angry, that was easy but using that anger effectively was the challenge. I had lost my ability to be angry in purpose for the right reasons to the right degree at the right time and in the right way.

The Tetrahedron, a representation of Fire. Associated with the Solar Plexus and the Ego. A force that mirrors the heart. This image shows the curved construct that creates the angles that thus begins the tetrahedra.

This is the false perception of duty to serve as protector never showing weakness instead replacing it with whatever the trigger and circumstance requires in order to return to safety. The gatekeeper of the inner self locked away never allowing anyone including me to pass and it was non-negotiable. *"Hearts become separated and dormant to protect the mind trapped inside so it is hidden away for all our life, but we have no knowledge of this. It is the greatest tragedy of our time."* My poles were shifting and I was moving randomly between the old and the new completely unaware. Polar shifts starts inside and manifests outside except I didn't know what that meant, what to look out for or how to deal with it. I had some idea from my research but I had no understanding of it. One thing I did figure out as I looked at myself and the resurfacing trauma it became clear this internal battle and its barriers of self-protection against allowing the trauma to re surface would become the war I would have to fight. But who was I fighting. This condition exists in every single one of us, there are no exceptions. I didn't realize the extent of the complexity of it all.

I wondered, would we make the same choices if we knew how this life really works. I'm not so sure we would. Consider…*"If you took a bus and found out it was the wrong bus you'd not take it again. Would you have taken it to begin with knowing it was the wrong bus?"* I make this example yet I struggled with the same poor relationships over and over each time thinking the end would be different. I was trapped in my own hypocrisy and bound by the bitterness of old. *"Consider what we could do with the lost time if we grew up knowing this."*

What I was searching for I wasn't going to find with this mindset. I was angry but anger wasn't going to help me here as it used to before. I needed another way. *"For only in the search for truth could my soul be stilled and the flame within be quenched"* Emerald Tablets. Slowly I began to cool my mind and body focusing instead on that beautiful voice and how it made me feel. I could never forget and I never wanted to forget. It was like dancing with pure love entangled in a moment I never wanted to end.

"Who was that voice? Where did that calm come from? What is the heart? Why am I always so angry and so easily frustrated? I can see some patterns so how do I fail to restrain myself even after knowing this. Why do I feel so out of place, even worse than before?

It's was hard to describe and share what I was experiencing. All those around me had assumed I'd lost my mind, at times I thought I was losing my mind because I was torn between the forgotten and this one light that was shining in the dark that I could not explain it for the life of me. I buckled under the pressure of the emotions more times than I could count. I was trying to express this confusing joy and calm and explaining it in fragments to help others see it but how does one explain something one does not understand. Only much later would I take this advice from the tablets..."*The wise man lets his heart overflow but keep silent his mouth."* It took a while to learn this though. I learnt that when one seeks truth for truth's sake often one must become invisible from the world and the self where the truth is largely absent, I think it was because the truth was absent in me.

I had found myself drifting in a dream of the real world slowly and quietly retracting inward to this mystical place that once I wanted nothing to do with. I was looking at everything from somewhere else like I had crossed a kind of invisible line. It's a strange place. I couldn't tell you where here was. More voices came with time cycling away as I slowly opened myself up to myself. Inner questions came with answers that I could trust. The wisdom it brought through its application allowed for a deeper perspective as I opened myself to this unknown. I had begun a dialogue with the voices I did not know the origins of, speaking to me about things I didn't know how to imagine, showing me things I never cared to learn growing up and was never taught by any elder. This is why I started taking things seriously. What was being shared had value and when applied without resistance always brought positive results. I, however, showed a lot of resistance because I struggled to reason with it all. I was too careful initially paying more attention to where this information came from as I was aware and never ignorant to the possibility that this might come from a dark place designed to deceive and mislead. Whilst I never aligned myself with any religion the skeptic in me remained aware of the presence of supposed good and evil because I didn't know any better. This was a great obstacle and took a long time to overcome. I had to get to know myself, all of me and align myself with a worthy Master Reference.

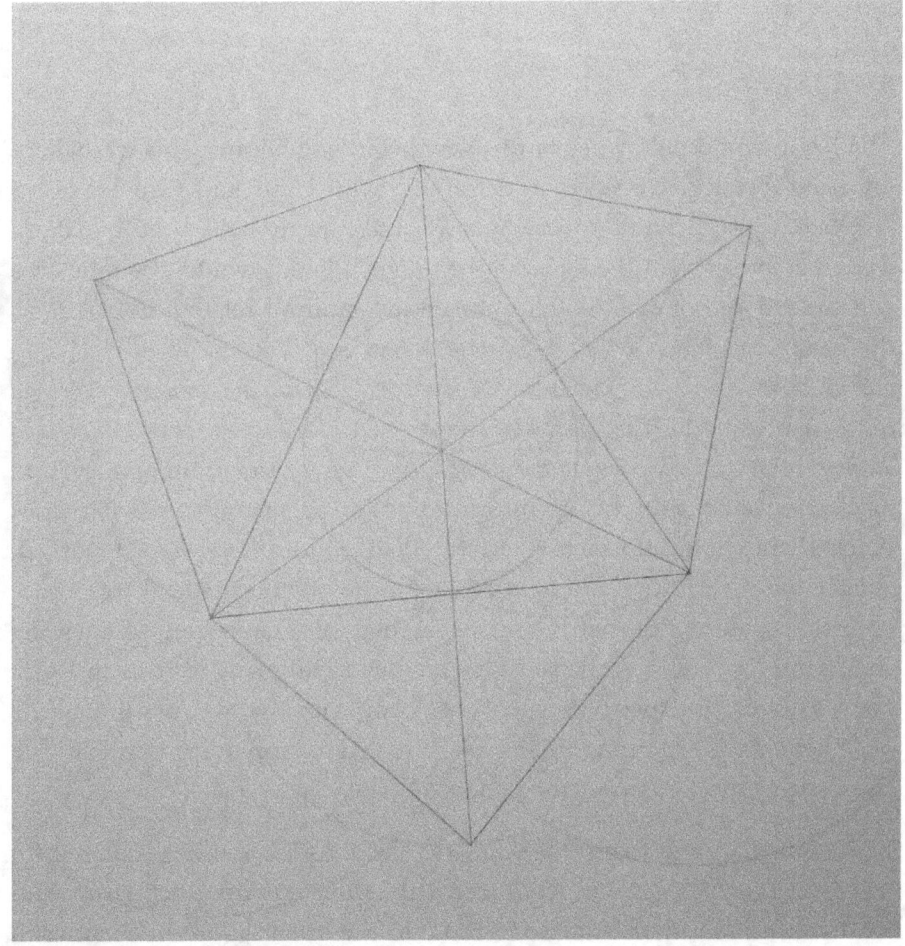

I regard this as the true Cube or hexahedron. It incorporates the angles that binds this world and the other as one in the moment,

separated by the perception of separation only and the differential between the default and perceived vibration. Expand the orientation and match this image to the axis that creates the orion nebula. Rotate and overlay and see the truth hidden in plain sight.

Root Down

The Root would be my key in this new beginning because this was where my fears dwelled. I needed to determine who I was and who I was no longer because I didn't know anymore, I always thought I did but there were massive gaps in the knowing I thought I had. I would close my eyes and see red and orange blotches. From my studies I related the colors to the chakra system *(Chakra is a Sanskrit term and it means "wheel" or "disk" and is derived from the root word "Chakra". Chakras are spinning wheels of energy/light. Chakras have the loving responsibility of taking in, incorporating and emanating energy to keep us functioning at optimal levels.)* I read up about it and discovered they may be symptoms of blocked energy. So what does blocked energy mean exactly because I had no idea how this all worked. What I did realize was if I could deal with the obvious issues I was aware of first I could dig deeper in and see if they were connected to anything else in any way. This made sense to me but I had many lessons to learn, many failures to experience and I was okay with that or so I thought. I had spent my life ignoring myself so I decided to stop doing that and give this dance with the moonlight a chance.

I was going to rise from the ashes of old. I found the beginnings of a new way as I began to work through some of my skepticism and frustrations instead of being triggered into the usual aggressive responses. This was not easy in the beginning because I was wired in a specific way and at times felt like I couldn't stop the engagements till it was done. I was used to having my frustrations dictate my actions regularly affecting others because I was unable to deal with our own triggers. I chose not to see the pain I caused and whilst many times I was truthful and accurate I had no empathy toward others and the truth became a tool of brutality I was only too happy to use.

There was no compassion in me and I was beginning to see that now. This raised a lot of guilt for the things I knew I did wrong. I was lost in my own fight, bound to my decisions which I believed at the time were right, always searching for the same justifications not caring to apologize. Even when I did it was cold and empty. My primary ability was to spin the wheel of guilt to work in my favor, it became a second skin and without these spinning wheels I didn't know how to function. Always insecure, never whole and I was guilty of worse. Admitting the dark inside that I was aware of took time. My apathy, the abortions, the deep-rooted depression and grief. The cheating and sleeping with married women. The pornography, greed, laziness and shaming people. The revenge I took to feed the bitterness inside. The things I ignored and done nothing about. My selfish pride and the need to always put myself first. I was guilty of it all. This bent me and at times I felt broken all over again but it was required to understand the purpose of my suffering as I stopped the wheels turning.

I thought I didn't fear anything till I started facing my real fears. Till the panic made me retreat and resist after. Till it almost killed me and till I almost killed myself in the madness of what I didn't understand, crossing barriers I didn't even know existed. This was all so new to me. I had never brought the inside out. I had never gone inside to search in this cold unknown. I didn't even have any real objective other than to repeat what happened that first time. *The experience is similar to standing underneath a positive stream of water like a shower, with one's head tilted backwards, allowing the water to run over your nose and mouth at the same time and trying to breathe. This results in panic. (Do not try this at home) Try and imagine then having to work your way through this destabilized emotional state maintaining composure and position of mind to access the spaces beyond.* The voice was right I was blind here. It's horrible but I had limited options at that time. I determined early on that using self-induced suffering would be a way to access the unaccusable and it did prove effective, it also took a lot out of me. I wouldn't allow myself to sit down for days, I would only eat the absolute minimum. I wouldn't sleep. I wouldn't drink anything. I only walked barefoot. I stopped speaking for extended periods. I stopped using my right hand and started using my left hand for everything. I pushed myself into the blackness. My feet would pain so badly. I didn't allow myself to treat the pain until I gave up something inside. I intentionally made my life uncomfortable because that's the only way I could break free from my comfort areas. I tortured myself into submission because I knew I was hiding things from myself. I knew that I did not have control of all of me. I knew this through the experience of forgetting things when on the verge of making breakthroughs. My mind was deleting on a moment to moment basis because of these spaces I had penetrated.

With my limited understanding I realized that I could control my conscious decisions but I had no control of my subconscious. That space was like hell and I was conscious of the hell inside of me. I was conscious of the demon I became and I was ready to rectify the imbalance even if it meant forcing that rectification when needed. In my arrogance I never thought of the consequences. I never considered that I was opening paths to the beyond. I was just trying to get everything out that I now know was harming me inside. I wasn't willing to wait till I died when I knew I wasn't walking this earth alive. I was a slave to the angels of today's world, lost in the lowest vibrations and I was releasing that negative energy into the world.

I wasn't born this way but I felt like I had inherited this disease and was setup to fail from the beginning. A part of me was still trying to blame someone, something. This would not excuse or justify the things I had done as I grew older. I was defined by what I didn't understand. It wasn't fair but then how would we define fair? Try explaining fairness to those who come from abusive homes and note abuse is not always sexual or physical. Often we forget the subtle nature unreasonable anger, parental moods, being absent claiming that there is not enough time to love the children you have brought into the world. Parents separating themselves from the example, teaching with the expectation that the child must follow saying…"Do as you are told not as I do." Parents in their own misery projects onto their children the anger and frustration that comes from their expectations not being met whether it's in the home or work, never including themselves as part of the problem. We as children never fully understanding that the parent's anger toward us has nothing to do with us yet most times we grow up in that dark shadow.

I chose this way too because I didn't admit that I sold a lie as the truth. Even when I had the real truth in I would not move and make the decisions that would set me free as though being imprisoned for all eternity is worse than the freedom beyond the bars I built. I had become the warden of my own prison and I protected that cell destroying all who came near. I was fueled by doubt, guilt, false empathy and fear rippling into the chaos that was the unconscious world I created masking myself as something I was not. This was the senselessness of my closed mind where my shadows ruled. As I was uncovering more and more about myself I wasn't happy and grew even more angry at everything. I had been standing at the dark door my whole life, haunted by not opening it and now that I had I was consumed with emotion and in my frustration, I abandoned everything.

I chose to indulge in some mind-bending mayhem riding into the sunset. I loved riding. Death and life and the throttle, concentration and release in the moments where time moves too fast to think so just don't think at all. As the years went by I stopped caring as much about living for tomorrow. I stopped caring about the worst that could happen and made peace with dying because nothing really mattered anymore. I would park along the beachfront with my bike in view and a beer in hand, mind on cruise control. In the silence of the madness the noisy bars never disturbed me.

Whilst I never had a problem communicating I rarely chose to speak to others. This occasion a voice whispered…"Are you afraid of falling?" I said…"Not since the first fall" She smiled and said…"You're brave" I replied…"No more brave than you are." Then I smiled softly as I realized…"I am brave so why won't I take a moment and be honest to myself? Why do I keep running away?" I was afraid and this was messing with all of me and rattling my crooked equilibrium. Several drinks and hours later I rode into the sunrise parking along the same stretch of beach. Gazing into the rising sun the sky changed that morning, a green light was seared into my sight as a voice spoke through the flames of the fire silently saying…"It is time to get started."

That morning I went home less doubtful than before. Without sleeping again I picked up a pen and paper and allowed the words to flow where ever my mind was willing to direct it but it wasn't my mind leading, it was something else. I was listening to music that reminded me of the pain from the years they occurred. This helped me. Many thoughts made its way to paper. I wrote and broke down again and again many times after and as the seasons passed the memories began to return one after the other. I never knew I felt so strongly about seemingly trivial things. I didn't know that it had caused me so much pain and broke my heart so badly that I had to close every door, that I could no longer utter any words of love. This wasn't how I remembered a lot of what had happened.

My anger had bent the truth inside and at times made it something else completely. I couldn't see through the mirror of my painful past, I didn't even know to look here. I didn't think this would go this way but then what rules were there for diving inward? The guidelines that spiritual teachers offer at times appear so abstract that its translation was lost in my interpretation. There were no directions, just like walking in that dark forest. Where I was could not be seen or heard, it could not be felt or smelt. How was I supposed to even comprehend it? *The Emerald Tablets* read… *"Know ye that the soul must be cleansed of its darkness before ye may enter the portals of light, though man may fall into darkness, always the light will shine as a guide, hidden in darkness, veiled in symbols, always the way to the portal will be found"* It seemed as though I had found a way to open up all be it using the combination of methods that may offend a purist. Waking up afterwards I felt lighter and somewhat more relaxed again. I went to the garden, had a sat and a small smile found its way to the surface. I usually kept what I was really thinking deep inside with a dead face, another mask I rested safely behind.

When you activate parts the dimensions of your mind you don't yet exist then the sacred geometry will begin to make more sense than it may ever do otherwise. Has the squares started moving yet? If it doesn't ask yourself what is blocking your flow? What has disconnected you?

"Meditate on the symbols I give he, keys are they though hidden from man"...Emerald Tablets

I had many veils that kept me safe and sedatives that kept me quiet. All of my habits were born from ignoring the bad. I had seen from the ancient texts and art that many past king's and pharaoh's bodies held traces of substance abuse. I questioned their kingships because it contradicted the true ancient teachings. I learnt the hard way that substances used without purpose can launch you into a linear path into the abyss and without stabilization you will fractal into the unknown spaces that are barred from man where insanity dwells and is perceived as the divine. *"Years later I too would come to learn that everything I did under the influence I would have to redo while being sober." That was a hard realization, an effect of the cause I was up until this moment, unaware of.*

Gateways follow the path of least resistance. Pain is a physical phenomenon, suffering is our psychological resistance to what happens. Events may create the physical pain, but they do not in themselves create suffering. Resistance creates suffering. Worry, anxiety and stress results when the mind resists what is. This was the problem to overcome. I had to resist less so I could push deeper, a little more each time. *"Man only exists on that which he resists, so earth must resist many else he existeth not." Emerald Tablets.* These gateways open only temporarily offering glimpses inward and not continuous thus is one of the greatest distortions and tragedies of the interpretation of the mighty wisdom. It stems from not knowing who we are. I didn't know who I was, not just as a human but beyond the limitations of the human, this unknown requires a courage to resist less. I was beginning to understand this. In a way it was changing me from within. I wasn't totally lost. I began to see a connection that was no longer beyond my once limited perception. This was purposeful because I could make my way back.

"Plumb the heart of all mystery" Mystery is Misery.

The geometry serves as keys unlocking the gateways of inner consciousness. Draw your own and they will become the keys of doors you do not know exists yet. These gateways can only be found when you free yourself and begin to flow within divine alignment. "Meditate on the symbols I give he, keys are they though hidden from man" Emerald Tablets

I had to release more to go deeper inside and acquire new clues and thoughts to lead my way. I knew when I had passed further in because my thoughts kept evolving. New memories kept re-surfacing. I never knew I thought so little of myself, this had to change. I was separated from so much of myself and I viewed the world as such. Piecing it together slowly allowed me to understand that my separation is divided by my conscious awareness and my growth experienced within the unified consciousness which is consciously expressing itself separately from another unified by the whole which is the fractal differential between Duality, Unity and Harmony. I was part of a greater all than I ever thought and thus I came to learn of my connection to all things, even a black rose. This was so far from anything I knew but it resonated with me and I began to see myself as more than just the root. I began to see myself as the stem, the branches, the leaves, the flower, the sand, sky, moon, and stars. This was profound. I had never seen myself this way and it felt right.

FRACTAL DEFINITION - A geometric equation / figure, each part has the same statistical character as the whole, infinite when applied inward and outward.

The universe is a multiverse of self-replication repeating over and over, in and out. Through these strange angles lay the dimensional gaps of consciousness through which you can penetrate into other spaces, 15deg is the key. A collective alignment based on KNOWING. That opens the gateway.

If you throw a stone in a still pond the first ripple is unaware of the ripples to come and what will come thereafter. That

I began to see a programming language that lies beyond the random nature of nature. An order that exists when we choose to look beyond the surface. These infinite ratios are not man-made and yet the same geometry exists in man. So too in ocean aquatics as in space and nature in all its beauty. This is vitally important but how could this be? One set of codex found everywhere and isn't man made? This is evidence of an active intelligence, a designer, but who was the designer? At this point it didn't matter that proof was simple enough for me, this order showed that the universe is not random, it is everything but random and yet is governed by the perception of random.

Phi (Φ = 1.618033988749895...), is simply an irrational number like pi (p= 3.14159265358979...) but one with many unusual mathematical properties. Unlike pi, which is a transcendental number, phi is the solution to a quadratic equation. Phi is the basis for the Golden Ratio, Section or Mean.

The ratio, or proportion, determined by Phi (1.618 ..... and continues to infinity) was known to the Greeks as the "dividing a line in the extreme and mean ratio" and to the Renaissance artists as the "Divine Proportion." It is also called the Golden Section, Golden Ratio and the Golden Mean.

Circle with a diameter of 1 and circumference of pi, 3.14 Phi, like Pi, is a ratio defined by a geometric construction. Just as pi (p) is the ratio of the circumference of a circle to its diameter, phi (Φ) is simply the ratio of the line segments that result when a line is divided in one very special and unique way.

The Fibonacci sequence is a set of numbers that starts with zero, followed by a one, and proceeds based on the rule that each number (called a Fibonacci number) is equal to the sum of the preceding two numbers. If the Fibonacci sequence is denoted F (n), where n is the first term in the sequence, the following equation obtains for n = 0, where the first two terms are defined as 0 and 1 by convention: F (0) = 0, 1, 1, 2, 3, 5, 8, 13, 21, 34...

In some texts, it is customary to use n = 1. In that case, the first two terms are defined as 1 and 1 by default, and therefore: F (1) = 1, 1, 2, 3, 5, 8, 13, 21, 34... but zero must be included as part of the sequence.

The Fibonacci sequence is named for Leonardo Pisano (also known as Leonardo Pisano or Fibonacci), an Italian mathematician who lived from 1170 - 1250. Fibonacci used the arithmetic series to illustrate a problem based on a pair of breeding rabbits: "How many pairs of rabbits will be produced in a year, beginning with a single pair, if in every month each pair bears a new pair which becomes productive from the second month on?" The result can be expressed numerically as: 0, 1, 1, 2, 3, 5, 8, 13, 21, 34...

Fibonacci numbers are of interest to biologists and physicists because they are frequently observed in various natural objects and phenomena. The branching patterns in trees and leaves, for example, and the distribution of seeds in a raspberry are based on Fibonacci numbers.

A Sanskrit grammarian, Pingala, is credited with the first mention of the sequence of numbers, sometime between the fifth century B.C. and the second or third century A.D. Since Fibonacci introduced the series to Western civilization, it has had a high profile from time to time.

The Fibonacci sequence is related to the golden ratio, a proportion (roughly 1:1.6) that occurs frequently throughout the natural world and is applied across many areas of human endeavor. Both the Fibonacci sequence and the golden ratio are used to guide design for architecture, websites and user interfaces, among other things.

In the Human it can be observed in the following ways, do note that not every individual has body dimensions in exact phi proportion but averages across populations tend towards phi and phi proportions.

Eyes: Equal spacing in the inner and outer edges of the eyes. Spaces between eyes and the eye whites are in the golden proportion. Eyes form a golden rectangle.

Teeth: Form a golden rectangle.

Ear: Has Fibonacci sequence formed in our ears? Helps hearing better. Also, the ear has phi proportions in the spiral of the ear.

The face is based on the golden ratio. From the top of the head to the bottom of the chin, it should be 16.8 inches on average. This is a phi proportion. There are 5 openings on the face. That is a Fibonacci number.

The Heart: The aorta has golden ratio proportions that helps give the heart optimum pump structure. The EKG pattern of the human heartbeat is in a phi relationship with heart rhythm.

DNA: DNA spirals have phi proportions. The DNA molecule measures 34 angstroms long by 21 angstroms wide for each cycle in the double helix.

Hands: Using the index finger as an example, from the tip to the base of the wrist, is larger than the preceding one by about the Fibonacci ratio of 1.618.

Feet: The foot has several proportions based on phi lines, including: The middle of the arch of the foot, the widest part of the foot, the base of the toe line and big toe, the top of the toe line and base of the "index" toe

Arms: The ratio of your forearm to your hand is 1.618 or the golden ratio.

Body Temperature: If you take 0.618 (phi proportion) of 37°C which is average human body temperature, you get 23°C or 73°F which is "perfect room temperature"

I was amazed that the same ratios found in the ocean and nature also existed in me, in us all. It is found everywhere and works in the weirdest ways.

Flower petals

The number of petals in a flower consistently follows the Fibonacci sequence. Famous examples include the lily, which has three petals, buttercups, which have five, the chicory's 21, the daisy's 34, and so on. Phi appears in petals on account of the ideal packing arrangement as selected by Darwinian processes; each petal is placed at 0.618034 per turn (out of a 360° circle) allowing for the best possible exposure to sunlight and other factors.

Seed heads

The head of a flower is also subject to Fibonaccian processes. Typically, seeds are produced at the center, and then migrate towards the outside to fill all the space. Sunflowers provide a great example of these spiraling patterns. In some cases, the seed heads are so tightly packed that total number can get quite high — as many as 144 or more. And when counting these spirals, the total tends to match a Fibonacci number. Interestingly, a highly irrational number is required to optimize filling (namely one that will not be well represented by a fraction). Phi fits the bill rather nicely.

Tree branches

The Fibonacci sequence can also be seen in the way tree branches form or split. A main trunk will grow until it produces a branch, which creates two growth points. Then, one of the new stems, branches into two, while the other one lies dormant. This pattern of branching is repeated for each of the new stems. A good example is the sneezewort. Root systems and even algae exhibit this pattern.

Shells

The unique properties of the Golden Rectangle provide another example. This shape, a rectangle in which the ratio of the sides a/b is equal to the golden mean (phi), can result in a nesting process that can be repeated into infinity — and which takes on the form of a spiral. It's called the logarithmic spiral, and it is found in many shapes of shells.

Spirally Galaxies

Not surprisingly, spiral galaxies also follow the familiar Fibonacci pattern. The Milky Way has several spiral arms, each of them a logarithmic spiral of about 12 degrees. As an interesting aside, spiral galaxies appear to defy Newtonian physics. As early as 1925, astronomers realized that, since the angular speed of rotation of the galactic disk varies with distance from the center, the radial arms should become curved as galaxies rotate. Subsequently, after a few rotations, spiral arms should start to wind around a galaxy. But they don't hence the so-called winding problem. The stars on the outside, it would seem, move at a velocity higher than expected a unique trait of the cosmos that helps preserve its shape.

Animal Bodies

Even our bodies exhibit proportions that are consistent with Fibonacci numbers. For example, the measurement from the navel to the floor and the top of the head to the navel is the golden ratio. Animal bodies exhibit similar tendencies, including dolphins (eyes, fins and tail all fall at Golden Sections), starfish, sand dollars, sea urchins, ants, and honey bees.

"How does it all work?" The beautiful geometry of nature is the same geometry drawn in this book. I even took time to measure plants and their growth to verify and it was so. I did the same with my own body and it was so. Even the pyramids of Giza incorporated these proportions with almost absolute accuracy. These achievements were created by a civilization that only had the use of ancient tools. Modern archeologists fail to explain the many anomalies present. Like precision cuts in materials too hard to be achieved by bronze tools. The alignments and proportions in relation to the earth and the moon as the pyramid is to earth, again provides evidence of the fractal. The geographical precision of its placement. The astronomical alignments and mimicking thereof. Its

longitudinal position and accuracy north to south is evidence of an understanding about the earth and the universe that far surpasses our comprehension. When you analyze the other alignments of other pyramid complexes around the earth it is more than simply a coincidence when we are told that these civilizations had no contact with each other, The tablets read…*"sent I the sons of Atlantis in many directions that by the womb of time wisdom may again rise in her children…"* There was something bigger here than I knew or anyone could explain but the symmetrical nature of the evidence was undeniable and I would follow the evidence rather than the words of man. The Emerald Tablets reads *"all is part of all, greater than we ever knew"* Something I was doing was aligning myself with a higher connection to the all. I was unlocking not only my prison but a gateway to a deeper understanding of our universe and the hidden world within.

"Built I the great pyramid patterned after the power of earth force burning eternally…" Emerald Tablets. Thoth the God of Wisdom claims he was the builder of the Great Pyramid today that credit goes to Khufu. I have interpreted this differently. From my research and experience I know that truth built the pyramids. A unified people with a singular purpose constructed the pyramids in the understanding of this truth. **I began to see that as with Fibonacci so it is with the human purpose searching and striving to align itself with the golden ratio ever closer to the knowing and living in the divine frequency.** This was a totally new way of thinking which made more sense to me than any of the previous world views and philosophies I had come across.

"Deep in earth's heart lies the flower, the source of the spirit that binds all in its form. Know ye that earth is living in body as though art alive in thy own form formed" **Emerald Tablets revealing the Multiverse**

"The flower of life is as thine own place of spirit and streams through the earth as thine flows through thy form, giving of life to the earth and its children, renewing the spirit from form unto form, this is the spirit that is the form of thy body, shaping and molding into its form" **Emerald Tablets**

In my evaluation I asked myself about the life I created in the outer world and how it reflected in my inner self with relation to the ratio of divine alignment. I tried to see the lessons being shown to me. To recognize and make sense of my behavioral cycles. How did I deal with arguments? Why do I even argue? Why are things drawn to me? Why do I attract the women I do? Why do they all resemble my mother? Everything was relevant or else it wouldn't continuously repeat in my life, this was the law of attraction, the principle of mind. I needed some time to understand this law and the other laws related to this.

Chapter 3

The law

I was able to uncover and understand in part the law of energy and the cosmic. The Hermetic Principles is connected to the Tablets via its author, Hermes who is believed to be an ancient incarnation of Thoth the author and creator of the Tablets. Later incarnations would include Enoch which was excluded from the mainstream Bible. *"Master of all arts and sciences, perfect in all crafts, Ruler of the Three Worlds, Scribe of the Gods, and Keeper of the Books of Life, Thoth Hermes Trismegistus—the Three Times Greatest was regarded by the ancient Egyptians as the embodiment of the Universal Mind. While in all probability there actually existed a great sage and educator by the name of Hermes, it is impossible to extricate the historical man from the mass of legendary accounts which attempt to identify him with the Cosmic Principle of Thought."* Manly P. Hall— *The Secret Teachings of All Ages*

Hermeticism is the school of ideas and systems that focuses on the pursuit of Gnosis, meaning the pursuit of empirical knowledge pertaining to spiritual mysteries. In a historical world where all major religions had gatekeepers to the spiritual experience, the Gnostics, and later Hermeticists rebelled in thought taking the pursuit of the mystical experience into their own hands and developed a way of thinking about the world that helped them communicate with and directly experience what they call *"a more visionary reality."* This was a problem as the gatekeepers to the spiritual experience ie the priests and the institutions they represented were no longer needed.

I would immerse myself in the study of this doctrine. These 7 Laws are some of the oldest and most influential systems of harmonious thinking. It claimed to broaden possibilities and aids one in the pursuit of a happier, more meaningful and longer life. It would prove a turning point in breaking the mold of my old way of thinking.

1. The principle of Mentalism - *All is mind, the universe is mental*
   This first principle embodies the truth that 'All is Mind.' Meaning, the Universe itself, at an underlying and foundational level, is Mental. That all phenomena of life, matter and energy of the material universe are thoughts of an infinite and universal, living Mind. Which means all things share a connection in the fact they exist within the Mind of 'THE ALL', as it is put, and therefore are all subject to the laws of created things. This Mental Universe, for the sake of experiment, could be explained as an infinite intelligence, and even the nature of consciousness itself. Creating a dialogue of thought which dances with thought. I found this most profound as it felt like I had been dancing with the many voices inside.

   The Principle of Mentalism, explains the nature of 'energy,' 'power,' and 'matter' as being subordinate to the Mind, as it shows up within ourselves and the pervading nature of all things. When you view everything you think, and therefore do, as an interaction of thought with thought, you develop an understanding of this first principle.

2. The law of Correspondence – *As above, so below. As below, so above. As within, so without. As without, so within.*
   This principle embodies the truth that there is always a correspondence between the laws and phenomena of various planes that manifest as being and life. Grasping this principle is what allowed me to deduce the hidden solutions to problems by looking at what exists a layer above, and below the problem, to see the patterns and shadow nature of what is in between the angles. There are planes and phenomena beyond our knowing, as we are limited to the spectrums of visible light (until we unlock further) and audible sound but by witnessing the patterns that do exist in our dimension we can deduce what may exist in higher and lower ones. Just as the knowledge of Geometry allows one to measure the cosmos and map its movements, as a dance of spheres and spirals. Observing the Principle of Correspondence, we can come to know the whole of the Universe by exploring the higher and lower nature of things,

which surround the mystery. We discover more of ourselves by experiencing and studying the world we are integrally a part of through the pursuit of Gnosis and its wisdom. The micro is in the macro, and vice versa, governed by but not limited to the default.

3. The Principle of Vibration – *Nothing rests everything moves, everything vibrates*
It explains that matter, energy, and even spirit, are simply varying rates of vibration (except for one, the stillness of the unknown unknown).
An example of this being frequency in which the seven octaves of music, tuned up 44 octaves, miraculously becomes the spectrum of visible light (passing through states of being the buzz pitch of insects, ultra-sound, plasma, ether, hyper sound, and even octaves of heat.) While they change manifestation, the vibrations maintain the same correspondence, the difference being only in measurement and energy as frequencies slide up the electromagnetic spectrum. At the highest rates of vibration the rate and intensity are so rapid it appears to be motionless, like a spinning wheel appearing stable. And at the lowest levels of vibration, objects move so slowly they appear to be totally at rest. Between these two, exist infinite manifestations all occurring at varying octaves of vibration, each with their own phenomena. It is believed that even thoughts have their own rate of vibration, and can be controlled like tuning an instrument, to produce various results for the aim of self and environmental mastery. I realized that if I could increase my understanding of vibration, frequency, harmony and resonance then that would change me at levels I could not yet comprehend.

4. The Principle of Polarity - *Everything is dual; everything has poles; everything has its pair of opposites; like and unlike are the same; Opposites are identical in nature, but different in degree; Extremes meet; all truths, are but half-truths; all paradoxes may be reconciled.*
This principle embodies the truth that "everything has its pair of opposites," "everything has two poles," and exists in a state of "duality" with Harmony being the zero-point collective. The true nature of this

principle is that "opposites are the same, only varying in degree and perspective." It explains that there are two poles in everything and that opposites are really only two extremes of the same thing. An obvious example being hot and cold—both being temperature, varying only in degree and that there is no clear crossover moment when hot stops being hot and starts being cold and vice versa with no absolutes on either end. This is relative to one's senses. The same can be said of 'light and darkness' 'hard and soft' 'big or small' and even 'love and hate.' With 'love and hate' there is no clear point where one emotion becomes another, or when it passes through 'like' 'dislike' or 'indifference.' All are merely our perceptions of the degree. And the principle of Polarity exists to explain these paradoxes. This principle is important because it suggests we can change the polarity of a degree of emotion, by recognizing it is the same and choosing the degree which best suits our needs. This is similar to rapid transitions in our psyche between love and hate, like and dislike, you can choose to experience these transitions by use of your willpower for the betterment of your life and others. The difference is not a hurdle to be surmounted, but two expressions of the same thing, differing only in degree, to choose between. This practice is the art of Mental Alchemy in pursuit of the magic invisible middle, the illusive space between the angles where the unknowable dwells.

The Principle of Rhythm - *Everything flows out and in, everything has its tides. All things rise and fall. The pendulum swing manifests in everything. The measure of the swing to the right is the measure of the swing to the left, rhythm compensates.*
Between the opposite poles of the principle of Polarity, is the pendulum swing of the principle of Rhythm. This principle embodies the truth that everything exists in a measured motion from here to there, moving in and out, swinging backward and forward, the cyclic nature of the rise and fall of all things, ebbing and flowing and never truly sitting still yet measurable to a degree in this predictable movement. Never stopping, always changing, and never changing. This principle controls the cycle of

life and death, creation and destruction, rise and fall, and of course manifests in our mental states.

When you are in tune with the Principle of Rhythm and understand that every mental state exists in Rhythm, always ebbing and flowing, you can learn to use this principle to your advantage by polarizing yourself to the degree you desire. Then, through awareness of this principle and how it manifests, holding yourself there to keep the pendulum from swinging you backwards to its extreme and thus stabilizing the self. Imagine going to an event that you know holds a lot of emotional significance for you, and checking in with yourself there. Knowing, you are experiencing a high and that this state is unsustainable, you can slot in time for transition to keep yourself from crashing, knowing the Principle of Rhythm is affecting you. Likewise, with times of stress and grief, giving yourself time to return to neutral before ramping back up again. Know that things you lose, will come back, and that things you own now, will disappear later. Being able to appropriate these smooth transitions can be the difference between days of recovery (mentally, physically, and emotionally) and smooth grace periods between times of intensity. This was something I needed to understand better because of the extreme nature of the way I had lived. I struggled knowing when to retreat and when to return and perfecting this was one of the many keys to self-mastery. Through heightened awareness gained by understanding this principle I determined that I could experience transcendental states of consciousness to rise above the swing of the pendulum. Rhythm would have an effect on me one way or another, but with awareness I could use it to propel myself forward and ride it back to recovery. All people who experience self-mastery do this to some degree, but those who exert their will upon this principle are able to act from a place of purpose as opposed to letting the pendulum swing them into reactivity. This was starting to make sense.

- The Principle of Cause & Effect - *Every cause has its effect; every effect has its cause; everything happens according to law' Chance is but a name for law not recognized' There are many planes of causation, but nothing escapes the law.*

This principle embodies the fact that there is a cause for every effect and an effect for every cause like the ripples in the pond. Nothing merely happens for no reason and that there is no such thing as chance. In harmony with the principle of Correspondence, there are higher planes dominating lower planes and nothing escapes the Principle of Cause & Effect. Nothing happens without explanation. The empowering use of this principle would be to make the conscious choice to rise above the plane of thought I currently occupied to become my own Cause and not just an Effect of others and the situations I found myself in. That is to say, be my own first mover as opposed to someone who merely reacts to circumstance. I know I am out of alignment with this principle, when I find myself feeling reactive and stressed, waking up only to handle and deal with the things that come my way. Instead, of going out of my own way to determine and create what I desire to experience. To put into action the first move, which will bring me the result I desire, not as a surprise, but a product of calculation, I had some work to do here.

- The Principle of Gender - *Everything has its masculine and feminine principles, gender manifests on all planes, like the polarities.*

This principle embodies the fact that both the masculine and feminine exist in all things. Not just in sex, but in the creative nature of all things and on all planes. In harmony with the principle of Correspondence, this means that the masculine and feminine exist not only in the physical plane, but also the mental, and the spiritual as well. The principle of Gender plays a role in all things generation, creation and regeneration. Nothing can come into being without the use of this principle. The masculine is the penetrative, assertive, progressive, conquering, explorative energy that drives progress. The feminine is the receptive, sacred, treasured, protective energy that maintains tradition and honors the priority of what is most important, while nourishing that which is most essential to life. Too much masculine energy, without a balance of feminine, leads to a linear growth of power to the extreme of reckless abandon where we lose perspective of what is most important and forget the principles which began the conquest in the first place. I was at fault of this many times over. While, too much feminine energy, without a balance of the masculine, leads to a life grounded so deeply in the present that our lives become determined by the cycles and external circumstance out of our favor. I was this product. All beings contain this great Principle within them, as two parts. Every male has feminine energy, and every female has masculine energy, this was something I had not known previously and took time to fully understand. In sex we see the interplay of these energies. In our moods, actions, attitudes, and personalities we see the dance of these energies within ourselves, now this statement made more sense to me. The most potent use of this principle is how Gender is responsible for creation, generation, and regeneration on the mental and spiritual planes, and not just the physical. True progress is possible through the balancing of the two energies of Gender in oneself, relationships, and environment. (This section does not mean that the author is opposed to LGBT, but the above example seeks to explain a spiritual point)

These mastered are the true law that should govern our reality as it once did. In the absence of understanding they bind us to the extremes of the dualistic expression of another seven which while relevant I chose to perceive differently.

The Seven Deadly Sins

1. Pride - is excessive belief in one's own abilities that interferes with the individual's recognition of the grace of God. It has been called the sin from which all others arise. Pride is also known as Vanity.
2. Envy - is the desire for others' traits, status, abilities, or situation.
3. Gluttony - is an inordinate desire to consume more than that which one requires.
4. Lust - is an inordinate craving for the pleasures of the body.

5. Anger - is manifested in the individual who spurns love and opts instead for fury. It is also known as Wrath.
6. Greed - is the desire for material wealth or gain, ignoring the realm of the spiritual. It is also called Avarice or Covetousness.
7. Sloth - is the avoidance of physical or spiritual work.

The Virtues

The Seven Contrary Virtues - humility, kindness, abstinence, chastity, patience, liberality, diligence

The Contrary Virtues were derived from the Psychomachia ("Battle for the Soul"), an epic poem written by Prudentius. Practicing these virtues is alleged to protect one against temptation toward the Seven Deadly Sins: humility against pride, kindness against envy, abstinence against gluttony, chastity against lust, patience against anger, liberality against greed, and diligence against sloth.

The Seven Heavenly Virtues - Faith, hope, charity, fortitude, justice, temperance, prudence

The Heavenly Virtues combine the five Cardinal Virtues: prudence, temperance, fortitude or courage and justice. With a variation of the theological virtues: faith, hope, and charity.

The Seven Corporal Works of Mercy - Continuing the numerological mysticism of seven, the Christian Church assembled a list of seven good works that was included in medieval catechisms. They are: feed the hungry, give drink to the thirsty, give shelter to strangers, clothe the naked, visit the sick, minister to prisoners, and bury the dead.

These can be found in almost all religions and cultures in varying forms. When we see the world in duality everything must be positive or negative. I took the above sins and virtues and converted it to energies as per the law seeing them as two opposite ends of the same thing. I questioned the accepted journey to one as the marriage of physical man and woman and looked at man and woman as part of the same being realizing it is not the sexual union of man and woman but energetically merging of the male and female energy within the self. This gives birth to the singular energy within the same self. The merging of positive and negative and the creation of what is to come. This was the understanding that I took from researching the many doctrines and may appear obvious but when one is oblivious to this it makes no sense because I didn't even know to think this way. I was like a forest full of dark trees, with the whistling winds haunting me as I searched for the roses under the pines.

These conclusions made sense on a theoretical level but before I could consider any of it I had to ask myself a few more important questions …"What's out of place? Where do my thoughts go that requires the suppression of eating? Why won't I tell anyone about the tears and the other darker appetites?" The shame it makes me feel and the guilt of it all that has become the fuel that drives me. "Why won't I tell the world I was hurt and that I am hurting? That I am afraid?" Instead I always mask my fears because of my pride, afraid of the judgment that I was sure would come. Who wants to speak of their true inner cravings or obsessive insecurities? In order to truly understand and live in the law I first needed to rectify the imbalance with myself like the lotus is the most beautiful flower, whose petals open one by one. But it will only grow in the mud. In order to grow and gain wisdom, first I had to have the mud, the obstacles of life and its suffering.

There was one that always hid away crawling through the dark corners of my mind. Bitterness should be right on top with the sins of man. I have been guilty many times spiraling out of control because of the cruel hand of my bitter mind. I would like to say that I've tried to be forgiving but that would be a lie. There were times in my life, whole years when it got the better of me. The ugliness turned me inside out. There was a certain satisfaction in bitterness, it gave me strength when I danced with it. Of all the monsters I invited in this was a real killer that had to be banished before I would find further answers that were buried beneath.

One can see its effects when one looks at those that struggle with debilitating ailments resulting from the habits it creates to suppress what is inside. The anger it generates must be hidden because we are so embarrassed and ashamed at a deep level within the unconscious. When we have the intellect and the confidence it becomes easy to turn that bitterness into a tool of destruction masking it as something other than the rotten darkness it is. With time we lose sight of its origins and take it as our own person. This is the dangerous tipping point of the pole shift. Without awareness we can no longer reverse the effects it has on the body, mind and spirit which manifest in varying ways. *"There through its lifetime that soul dwells in bondage..."* Emerald Tablets It is easy to see for most cannot control the body's automotive responses when triggered including myself. I noticed in myself how my eye would twitch and I would bite my teeth at times when I was trying to maintain my composure during difficult situations but inside I would say…"I will hurt you for this, I will take from you what you have taken from me. I don't know how yet, but give me time. A day will come when suddenly your joy will turn to ashes in your mouth and you'll know the debt is paid." I was in a constant battle to keep inside what I did not want the world to see. I hurt others because I was hurt…"Was I always like that or did we become that?" I wondered when I looked at my actions vs my suppressions. "I may have rationalized the actions I took by the principles I believed in yet why was I suffering? What inside has caused this suffering to begin with? Who was I really destroying?" Something inside was badly out of place.

I realized that if these issues were plaguing me then they were plaguing everyone in some way who was in my life and have been since previous generations. I was projecting my reality and it became apparent that collectively we have all been here for a long time trying to rectify the imbalance of histories past. We become what we become through our own doing because we are unaware and have never really learnt to communicate what truly lies inside. Worse is we live in a system today that promotes suppression through convenience and ignorance, which further binds the degeneration of the individual and the collective, and this all was starting to make sense.

I began to evaluate people not as humans but as energies, like charged particles we would normally study under microscopes, at a macro fractal level we too are charged energies no different from the cells in our body. This had a big effect. Seeing how I and my inner energy was the same as another inherently whilst appearing different on the surface. Seeing people in their homes and the way they conduct themselves claiming one thing yet doing another. Equally their partners doing the same and so the children doing the same also. I began to see the hypocrisy within myself more clearly. It is only through

Bring forth everything inside and what you bring forth will save you. From the gospel of Thomas. Release, set yourself free from yourself. What you do not bring forth will end a life that never began. This is the principle of purpose and it is the key to unlocking what is inside of us hidden way and lost. A fractal of infinity. The gift of life.

pole shifts that one can truly consider oneself not as another and yet equally as the other because all these energies are always flowing through us. I realized the power of tolerance through this understanding even though I myself was not very tolerant. I also realized that being neutral doesn't make one neutral in the same way how cars' wheels seem to stand still in certain lighting conditions, doesn't mean it's still and yet, it appears still. This phenomenon is known as the "wagon-wheel" effect. Like most people, you're accustomed to seeing the wagon-wheel effect in movies or TV, its explanation is fairly straightforward: Cameras record footage not continuously, but by capturing a series of images in quick succession, at a specified "frame rate." With many movie cameras, that rate is 24 frames per second. When the frequency of a wheel's spin matches the frame rate of the camera recording it (say, 24 revolutions per second), each of the wheel's spokes completes a full revolution every 1/24 seconds, such that it ends up in the same position every time the camera captures a frame. The result is footage in which the wheel in question appears motionless: So when a wheel seems to spin in a direction opposite its actual rotation, it is because each spoke has come up a few degrees shy of the position it occupied when it was last imaged by the camera. This is sometimes referred to as the reverse-rotation effect. If the spoke over-shoots, the wheel will appear to rotate in the right direction, but very, very slowly. Our eyes work in the same way. This is how I describe the collective charge of a human.

"I know this is a little cryptic but consider how would you know the difference between one thing and another that seemed absolutely identical? Wouldn't they then be identical? Why then do we argue with that which we are inside of?" The confusion of this led me to consider another beer but for once I chose not to drink. Instead I went for a walk. I felt out of place walking the path I normally ran noticing new things in the old I had never seen before, the details I didn't know existed and never thought to look for. All the colors that

surrounded me suddenly took on a new meaning. Like a dream in a place I'd never been before. "I was awake, alive, hardly." I saw a flower that was so beautiful and yet so simple. It sent a calm through me as the voice reappeared, that beautiful voice from before. My eyes welled up and I began to lose my breath. "Welcome back my dear Jonathan. Try to let your heart be still and the confusion rest. There is beauty in all things, whether a rose or the thorns that sometimes surround it, there is a lesson in both. Listen to the winds and the trees they have something to say. Slow down, you are missing the magical moments because you are rushing from one thing to another. You will never see what's right in front of you this way. You are so hard on yourself all the time. Would you consider being kinder to yourself? You cannot feel when you are still bound to this way. You must be free first then you will see as you begin to feel. Look down the answers are below."

This silent voice spoke in a way that only love can speak without words. I didn't know what love was but love should feel this way. I listened to the voice because I knew it was the truth. I still didn't treat myself and others well. I would rather turn to self-torture than be patient enough to allow myself to find the safety to release. I did terrible things that I didn't know how to forgive myself for and blamed others, taking revenge for what I believed was done to me. I destroyed my children, walked out on my family and pushed away everyone before they had a chance to show that they cared. I broke others that didn't deserve it and doing nothing to those who did. I shouted out loud that day…"I can't live like this anymore….I won't live like this anymore." In this moment, a great flash of light blinded my vision…"What the hell is going on?" I wondered as a voice spoke in silence…"Welcome, I have been expecting you.

The geometry starts using only curves, no straight lines, only the proportions that comes from divine expansion. The angles represents our false perceptions of the reality we know. Light moves in curves when it moves in curves. Breaking free from the angles allows us to see the light. The angles are a position of mind, as is all things.

Follow me I will show you the way. The ocean is the water of emotion incarnate. It loves, hates and weeps. It defies all attempts to capture it with words and rejects all shackles. No matter what you think or say, it holds more than you know and gives more than it shows."

This voice was different. What did it mean? What exactly did I just experience? I was unsure but there was no going back. Deep inside I know what I had experienced and from within the silence I heard…"Sometimes you should just stop trying to make sense of everything!" I was still anchored to the old world. I had never experienced the waters of the real. I was still dancing in the moonlight of the misty forest. It was time to move across these waters.

Deeper research and understanding

I needed to put more effort in, so I put myself to study yet again searching for a deeper understanding of everything I was experiencing. Revisiting the ancient teachings with a new perspective allowed me to see into the hidden codex of the written words and the minds of the authors who had thought them. Like the roots expanding I continued to learn and grow from both the studies and the applications in the real world. The results proved the teaching's accuracy, and this helped me deal with my doubts. It allowed me to find new symmetry between totally unrelated doctrines from cultures who had no contact to each other and existed at different times in history and even today still frown upon each other. I merged the alchemical teachings with the Hindi chakra system for self-transformation theorizing at the time that the true alchemical intention was not turning lead into gold but instead transforming the self from nothing into everything.

I aligned myself and my intentions with the virtues of the MA'AT *(Maat, also known as Ma'at or Mayet, was a female goddess in the ancient Egyptian religion who represented truth, justice, balance and morality. The daughter of the Egyptian sun deity Ra and wife of the moon god, she served a kind of spirit of justice to the Egyptians. She decided whether a person would successfully reach the afterlife, by weighing their soul against her feather of truth, and was the personification of the cosmic order and a representation of the stability of the universe. The earliest writings where she is mentioned date back to the Old Kingdom of Egypt.)* These virtues are relevant in all cultures/religions in different ways as I've shown earlier through the Hermetic Law, Sins and Virtues. Only the names of these cultures and religions differ. I would have to answer the 42 questions in this life as was done in the afterlife by the ancients, this was my objective, but I had a huge mountain in front of me that would not step aside, there was work to do.

The 42 read: I honor virtue. I benefit without violence. I am none violent. I respect the property of others. I affirm that all life is sacred. I give offerings that are genuine and generous. I live in truth. I hold sacred those objects that are consecrated to the divine. I speak the truth. I eat only my fair share. I speak words of good intent. I relate in peace. I honor animals as sacred. I can be trusted. I care for the earth. I keep my own council. I speak positively of others. I remain in balance with my emotions. I am trustful in my relationships. I hold purity in high esteem. I spread joy. I do the best I can. I communicate with compassion. I listen to opposing opinions. I create harmony. I invoke laughter. I am open to love in various forms. I am forgiving. I am non-abusive. I act respectfully of others. I am non-judgmental. I follow my inner guidance. I speak without disturbing others. I do good. I give blessings. I keep the waters pure. I speak with optimism. I praise truth. I am humble. I achieve with integrity. I advance through my own abilities. I embrace the all. There was a lot of work to do.

Aligning these virtues with the chakra system showed its connection to the tablets...

"First and most mighty, Lord of Lords the infinite 9, over the other from each the lord of the cycles, 3, 4, 5, and 6, 7, 8, (totals 7) each with his mission, each with his power, guiding, directing the destiny of man. There sit their mighty and potent, free from all time and space"

"Seven are the mansions of the house of the Mighty. Three guards the portal of each house from the darkness. Fifteen the ways that lead to Duat. Twelve are the houses of the Lords of Illusion. facing four ways, each of them different. Forty and Two are the great powers, judging the Dead who seek for the portal. Four are the Sons of Horus, Two are the Guards of East and West of Isis, the mother who pleads for her children, Queen of the Moon, reflecting the Sun."

These energies would prove most influential when the understanding thereof was correctly applied. Many speak of different chakra systems in ways that can become very complex, so I tried to make it as simple as possible. Below lists the chakras and their inner and outer nature associated in the real-world conditions. Consider it carefully as I did, it helped me understand or ease my sinus and asthma which crippled me for most of my life. We will use the seven system, know that the system works seven by two inner and outer (like the sins and virtues), zero to nine in the divine order with zero as 1. The other systems and colors will come as they are unlocked.

Root chakra (color red, soft red in its divine true color) Platonic earth
I AM
Security, grounding foundation
FOODS - Think Healthy red veg and fruit: apples, red peppers, plums, grape fruit, tomatoes.
Deals with your fears, issues relating to survival, money, food, sense of belonging, will to live, lack of trust, (free yourself from your fears) afraid to take action
BODY – constipation (and related ailments), colon, prostate (in men)
The root chakra provides the foundation on which we build our life. It supports us in growing and feeling safe into exploring all the aspects of life. It is related to our feeling of safety and security, whether it's physical or regarding our bodily needs or metaphorical regarding housing and financial safety. To sum it up, the first chakra questions are around the idea of survival and safety. The root chakra is where we ground ourselves into the earth and anchor our energy into the manifest world.

What happens when the first chakra is imbalanced? At the emotional level, the deficiencies or imbalance in the first chakra are related to: Excessive negativity, cynicism, eating disorders, greed, avarice, illusion, excessive feeling of insecurity. Living in survival mode constantly.

For a person who has imbalance in the first chakra, it might be hard to feel safe in the world and everything looks like a potential risk. The desire for security dominates and can translate into concerns over the job situation, physical safety, shelter, health. A blocked root chakra may turn into behaviors ruled mainly by fear. On the same line, when the root chakra is overactive, fear might turn into greed and paranoia, which are extreme forms of manifestation of imbalance in the first chakra. Issues with control over food intake and diet are related to it.

2. Sacral chakra (color orange) platonic water
- I FEEL
- The ability to accept others, new experiences, creative expression, sexual expression, fantasies
- FOODS – oranges, butternut, pumpkin, orange chillies, carrots, grape fruit, oranges, sweet melon DRINK LOTS OF WATER
- Emotions, sexuality, intimacy, quality of love and sexual energy (these must be released and transmuted to creative none body expression)
- BODY – lower abdomen urinary track system, ovarian/reproductive system (for women)

The most common location for the sacral chakra is just below the navel, at the center of your lower belly. In the back, it's located at the level of the lumbar vertebrae. Other noteworthy locations described in different systems, expand its location to the genital area, especially at the level of ovaries for women and the testicles for men.

The sacral chakra is associated with the realm of our emotions. It's the center of our feelings and sensations. It's particularly active in our sexuality and the expression of our sensual and sexual desires. Motivated by pleasure, it's the driving force for the enjoyment of life through the senses, whether it's auditory, through taste, touch, or sight. Opening your sacral chakra allows you to "feel" the world around and in us. As such, it's an important chakra at the foundation of our feeling of well-being. This was a problem for me and would prove to be a difficult hurdle to overcome as time cycled on. The second chakra is instrumental in developing flexibility in our life. Associated with the water element, it's characterized by movement and flow in our emotions and thoughts. It supports personal expansion and the formation of identity through relating to others and to the world.

When the sacral chakra is balanced, the relationship with the world and other people is centered on nurturing, pleasure, harmonious exchange.

Imbalance in the sacral chakra can manifest as: Dependency, co-dependency with other people or a substance that grants you easy access to pleasure. Here again I was guilty of over indulgence. Being ruled by your emotions. The opposite: Feeling numb, out of touch with yourself and how you feel. Overindulgence in fantasies, sexual obsessions. Or the opposite: Lack of sexual desire or satisfaction. Feeling stuck in a particular feeling or mood

3. Solar Plexus Chakra (color Yellow) platonic fire
- I WILL
- Will, personal power, Taking responsibility for one's life, taking control, Mental abilities, the intellect, Forming personal opinions and beliefs, making decisions, setting the direction, Clarity of judgments, Personal identity, personality, Self-assurance, confidence, Self-discipline, Independence
- Ego, negative, talk too much, act too little
- BODY - Upper abdomen, stomach, poor digestion, big appetite, blood pressure
- FOODS – bananas – pineapple – yellow pepper – avocado

The third chakra is located at the solar plexus level, between the navel and the lower part of the chest. That's why it's often referred to as the "solar plexus chakra." Some traditions place it more loosely in the navel area. Derived as the director of negative and is associated with the ego. Closely connected to the digestive system, especially the gastric and hypogastric plexus, its main function is to help transform matter into energy to fuel your body, but what fuel is the ultimate question. It governs metabolism and is commonly associated with the pancreas.

On one side, a balanced solar plexus chakra makes it easy to find balance between your personal power and harmonious relationships with others; on the other side, an imbalanced third chakra could undermine your self-esteem and social life.

When the Solar Plexus chakra is balanced, you may be assertive and exert your will in a way that leads to the expected results somewhat effortlessly. Have harmonious relationships with your surroundings.

Imbalances in the third chakra can manifest as: Excessive control and authority over your environment and people, or the opposite in case of deficiency or blocked energy: Feeling of helplessness, irresponsibility, being obsessed with minute details, seeing life through a filter of plus and minuses while losing sight of the whole picture. Being manipulative, misusing your power, lack of clear direction, lack of purpose or ambition, making plans or having a lot of ideas without finding efficient ways to realize them

MIRROR (Pole Shift)

4. Heart chakra (deep green, emerald green) Platonic Air/Love
- I LOVE
- The ability to love, inner peace, above the heart and in center, compassion, mercy, gratitude
- Grief, self-pity, fear of intimacy, anger etc.
- BODY – heart, thymus, lungs, immune system, circulatory system

- FOODS – kiwi – broccoli – kale – grapes - avocado

The most commonly accepted location for the fourth chakra is at the center of the chest, between the breasts. It's slightly to the left of the actual organ of the heart. That's why it's commonly referred to as the "heart chakra".

As the fourth energy center, it's important to remember that it is multidimensional and is energetically represented with a front going through the center of the chest, and a back going through the spine between the shoulder blades.

Because of its location, the heart chakra is associated to the cardiac system and the lungs. These organs are interdependent and rely on air and breathing to function properly. The gland associated with the heart chakra is the thymus, which is in charge of regulating the immune system.

The main meanings or functions associated with the heart chakra are: Love for oneself and others, relating, relationships, compassion, empathy, forgiveness, acceptance, transformation, change, ability to grieve and reach peace, compassionate discernment, and center of awareness and integration of insights. In me all of these aspects needed attention.

When the heart chakra is open, you may feel being deeply connected, the harmonious exchange of energy with all that is around you, and the appreciation of beauty which I was beginning to experience in its infancy. However, when there's a blockage in the heart chakra, you may experience difficulties in your relating with others, such as excessive jealousy, codependency, or being closed down and withdrawn which I also had problems with.

The fourth chakra connects the lower and upper chakras. In other words, the heart chakra acts as a center of integration of earthly matters and higher aspirations. Far from seeing these energies as separate, the experience of the heart integrates them effortlessly and harmoniously.

Love experienced through the fourth chakra is not just about romance, but about going beyond the limitations of the ego and personal preoccupations to open up more fully to compassion and acceptance of all that is, as it is. When we live from our heart and our heart energy is opened and balanced, we can see clearly and position ourselves in any situation, no matter how challenging it is, with discernment and compassion, this would be the master key.

The heart chakra is also a center through which we experience beauty in life. Seeing the world through a balanced fourth chakra is being in a state of openness and acceptance that brings us in touch with our world and ourselves in profound and fulfilling ways.

5. Throat chakra (color Blue, magic blue, turquoise, aqua marine) Platonic Sound
- I SPEAK
- Ability to communicate truth, express yourself with humility kindness and empathy, to not be silent when evil is spoken, to have the courage to speak up when no one else will
- BODY - Thyroid, teeth, vocals,
- FOODS- use green foods here an open heart speaks the truth
  The Throat chakra is the fifth chakra. Located at the center of the neck at the level of the throat, it is the passage of the energy between the lower parts of the body and the head. The function of the Throat chakra is driven by the principle of expression and communication. It's important to remember that this chakra is also multidimensional and is often represented as going out of the front of the throat, and going in the back at a slight upward angle. This chakra is related to the element of sound. Through the throat, sound is propagated into the air and its vibration can be felt not just in our ears, but also in our whole body. It is an important instrument of communication and expression but equally silence here is of great profit. The Throat chakra is associated to the pharyngeal and brachial plexus and is connected to the mouth, jaws, tongue, pharynx and

palate. It's is also linked to the shoulders and the neck. The gland associated with the fifth chakra is the thyroid, which regulates the processing of energy in the body through temperature, growth, and in large parts, metabolism.

Another function of the throat chakra is to connect you to spirit as it is one of the zero points. Because of its location, it's often seen as the "bottleneck" of the movement of energy in the body. It sits just before the upper chakras of the head. Opening the throat chakra can greatly help align your vision with reality and release pressure that may affect the heart chakra that is located just below. The throat chakra is associated with the etheric body, which holds the blueprint or perfect template of the other dimensions of the light body. It's an important reference point to align all the energies through the whole chakra system.

The Throat chakra is associated with the following psychological and behavioral characteristics: Expression, in particular ability to express your truth, to speak out. Communication, whether it's verbal or non-verbal, external or internal. Connection with the etheric realm through inner silence, the subtler realms of spirit and intuitive abilities. Propensity to create, projecting ideas and blueprints into reality. Realizing your vocation, purpose. Good sense of timing

The Throat chakra is about the expression of yourself: Your truth, purpose in life and creativity. Note that this chakra has a natural connection with the second chakra, center of emotions and creativity as well. The throat chakra's emphasis is on expressing and projecting the creativity into the world according to its authenticity and truth.

A blocked throat chakra can contribute to feelings of insecurity, timidity, and introversion. On the other end of the spectrum, an overactive throat chakra may also lead to gossiping, nonstop talking, and being verbally aggressive or mean. It can seem as though the filter between the discourse you have in your mind and what comes out of your mouth is not working or missing entirely.

When the throat chakra has an imbalance, it can manifest as: act of control over one's speech; speaking too much or inappropriately; not being able to listen to others. Excessive fear of speaking. Small, imperceptible voice. Not being able to keep secrets, to keep your word. Telling lies. On the opposite side, a closed throat chakra might manifest as excessive secretiveness or shyness. Lack of connection with a vocation or purpose in life.

6. Third Eye (color Indigo, it is actually a lot softer than indigo) Platonic Etheric water
- I SEE
- The ability to focus on the big picture, Intuition, imagination, ability to think and make decisions,
- BODY – pituitary gland, eyes sinus
- FOODS – granadilla, red grapes, plums, passion fruit, berries,
- Illusion, ignorance – check for headaches runny noses – head colds

The location for the sixth chakra is between the eyebrows, slightly above at the bridge of your nose. It can also be described as being located behind the eyes in the middle of the head.

In yogic metaphysics, the third eye or Ajna chakra, is the center where we transcend duality – the duality of a personal "I" separate from the rest of the world, of a personality that exists independently from everything else. As Harish Johari says, "a yogi who has passed through the Vishuddha Chakra at the throat to the Ajna Chakra transcends the five elements and becomes freed (mukta) from the bondage of time-bound consciousness. This is where the I-consciousness is absorbed into super-consciousness." The third eye chakra is most commonly represented with the color purple or bluish purple. The auric color of third eye chakra energy can also be seen as translucent purple or bluish white. Rather than by its color, it is characterized by the quality of its luminescence or soft radiance that reminds us of the moon light. I struggled to understand this because of my lack of spiritual or metaphysical connection to anything.

The Third eye chakra is associated to the pineal gland in charge of regulating biorhythms, including sleep and wake time. It's a gland located in the brain that is a center of attention because of its relationship with the perception and effect of light and altered or "mystical" states of consciousness. It's positioned close to the optical nerves, and as such, sensitive to visual stimulations and changes in lighting. The third eye chakra is an instrument to perceive the subtler qualities of reality. It goes beyond the more physical senses into the realm of subtle energies. Awakening your third eye allows you to open up to an intuitive sensibility and inner perception which I was lacking. Because it connects us with a different way of seeing and perceiving, the third eye chakra's images are impossibly hard to describe verbally. It puts us in touch with the intangible more closely. Third eye visions are also often more subtle than regular visions: They may appear a bit "blurry", ghost-like, cloudy, or dream-like. Sometimes however, the inner visions might be clear like a movie playing in front of your eyes. Sustaining awareness of third eye chakra energy might require focus and the ability to relax into a different way of seeing. When we focus our mind and consciousness, we can see beyond the distractions and illusions that stand before us and have more insight to live and create more deeply aligned with our highest good. The third eye chakra is associated with the archetypal dimensions, as well as the realm of spirits.

When the Third eye chakra has an imbalance, it can manifest as: Feeling stuck in the daily grind without being able to look beyond your problems and set a guiding vision for yourself which seemed to have become my daily routine. Overactive third chakra without support from the rest of the chakra system may manifest as fantasies that appear more real than reality which I also wondered about considering some of the experiences I was having, indulgence in psychic fantasies and illusions. Not being able to establish a vision for oneself and realize it. Rejection of everything spiritual or beyond the usual. Not being able to see the greater picture. Lack of clarity. I would have to dig deep here to expand my mind past my own limitations.

7. Crown Chakra (violet, also White Lavender, pink lavender) Platonic Etheric Fire
- I UNDERSTAND
- FRUITS – beetroot, eggplant, dragon fruit, berries, cauliflower, cabbage,
- BODY – top of head – brain – nervous system
- Ability to carry out ideas in a practical way, cosmic connection, seeing the connection of all things, been connected to all, feeling that connection, KNOWING, this is where wisdom lays also this is where the HYPER EGO dwells,

  Located at the top of the head, it gives us access to higher states of consciousness as we open to what is beyond our personal comprehensions and visions. The function of the Crown chakra is driven by consciousness and gets us in touch with the universal. The crown chakra is most commonly represented with the color white, although it can also be depicted as deep purple. The auric color of crown chakra energy can also be seen as gold, white, or clear light.

The Crown chakra is primarily associated to the pituitary gland, and secondarily to the pineal and the hypothalamus. The hypothalamus and pituitary gland work in pair to regulate the endocrine system. Because of its location, the crown chakra is closely associated with the brain and the whole nervous system. Note that energetically, the seventh chakra has a connection with the first chakra, as they both are at the extremities of the chakra system.

The crown chakra is associated with the following psychological and behavioral characteristics:

The crown chakra is associated with the transcendence of limitations, whether they are personal or bound to space and time. It is where the paradox becomes norm, where seemingly opposites are one. The quality of awareness that comes with the crown chakra is universal. As we are immersed in the energy of the crown chakra, we feel a state of union with all that is. This chakra allows access to the upmost clarity and enlightened wisdom. It can be described as the gateway to the cosmic self or the divine self, to universal consciousness.

When the Crown chakra has an imbalance, it can manifest as: Being disconnected to spirit, constant cynicism regarding what is sacred. On the opposite side, an overactive crown chakra could manifest as a disconnection with the body. Living in your head, being disconnected from your body and earthly matters. Obsessive attachment to spiritual matters. Closed-mindedness. All of these symptoms were present in me and I was becoming more aware of the impact it had on my life.

For the sake of understanding the chakra colors it is important to know how the colors mix when using liquids and light.

With light

- Green and red makes yellow
- Green and blue makes cyan
- Red and blue makes magenta
- Red blue and green makes white

With liquids

- Blue and yellow makes green
- Blue and red makes purple
- Yellow and red makes orange
- Blue(cyan), magenta(red), yellow makes black NOT WHITE

I had a profound realization. You may try this and see if you make your thumb zero and the other one nine then your two small fingers are four and five. Then zero, four, five and nine is part of the same circle. I was beginning to see the world from a new perspective and it was changing my perspective of the world I knew. Knowing this is important is of great value.

I looked at the varying pathways within the ancient texts and the energies it manifested as and related it to the energies of the people I had met in my life including myself. It made for a new understanding of who was who if they were not simply random.

"Rule they forever with infinite wisdom, bound yet not bound to the dark Halls of Death. Life they have in them, yet life that is not life, free from all are the Lords of the ALL. Forth from them came forth the Logos, instruments they of the power o'er all. Vast is their countenance, yet hidden in smallness, formed by a forming, known yet unknown."

"THREE holds the key of all hidden magic, creator he of the halls of the Dead; sending forth power, shrouding with darkness, binding the souls of the children of men; sending the darkness, binding the soul force; director of negative to the children of men."

"FOUR is he who loses the power. Lord, he, of Life to the children of men. Light is his body, flame is his countenance; freer of souls to the children of men."

"FIVE is the master, the Lord of all magic - Key to The Word that resounds among men."

"SIX is the Lord of Light, the hidden pathway, path of the souls of the children of men."

"SEVEN is he who is Lord of the vastness, master of Space and the key of the Times."

"EIGHT is he who orders the progress; weighs and balances the journey of men."

"NINE is the father, vast he of countenance, forming and changing from out of the formless."

To access these energies at this level would require an understanding of the alchemical order of transmutation and became the process I used to apply the code within the Tablets relating it to the understanding of the chakras above.

- Calcination (Aries)
- Burn off excess

Root
Base of spine
Dissolution (cancer – cleansing)
Immerse in the rejected parts of the mind
Bringing the buried to the surface
Allowing new energy flow
Opening of new energy channels
Separation (Scorpio)
Filtration
Processing
Rediscovery (previously rejected by male mind)
Decides what to discard
Keep letting go of restraints
Gives birth to new energy
Physical renewal
Conjunction (Venus – heart)
Empowerment of true self
Union – merging of male female energies
Union of whole being
After achieving the self knows what needs to be done to achieve lasting enlightenment
Look out for synchronicities
Fermentation (Capricorn) petrification of hermaphrodite
Death and resurrection to new level of being
New life, the product of conjunction
To strengthen and ensure survival (hold and lock the vibration)
Fermentation begins with the inspiration of spiritual power providing new energy to the self
Intense prayer (know who you praying to and why, do not pray in separation) / affirmation
Desire for mystical union
Breakdown of personality
Meditation

- Inner self therapy
- Rising of energy to the throat indicates an evolution of life to higher levels of consciousness.
- Distillation (Virgo)
- Is the purification of the unborn self
- All that we truly are and truly will be
- It is the raising of the life force from the lower regions of the self eventually becoming a light of power in unity
- Agitation and sublimation of physical forces is necessary to ensure no traces of the ego remains (test yourself) or deeply immerged self are incorporated into the next phase.
- Personal distillation consists of a variety of introspective techniques that raise the level of the physic (as expressed in previous writings) to the highest level possible, free from the emotions cut off even from personal identity (to know everything you must become nothing)
- Coagulation (Taurus)
- Is the precipitation or sublimation of the purified ferment of distillation (the result of the cause – what you put in is what you get out)
- A new confidence beyond all things
- A permanent vehicle of consciousness that embodies the highest aspiration and evolution of the spirit
- Incarnates and releases the ultimate material of the soul and astral body which is also referred to as the greater or philosophers stone
- Allows for existence on all levels of reality
- The knowing that comes from the process of growing

Alchemical merge

1. NIGREDO (BLACK) eliminate all ideas and limitations, rebirth can only take place when all is cleared away
2. ALBEDO (WHITE) pure and receptive spiritual stage (establishment of self-control) allowing growth and expansion of consciousness
3. RUBEDO – (RED) puts ideas to practice, valuable knowledge must NOT remain idle, practice brings enlightenment

The application of the above was simplified even further because comprehension requires simplification.

Imagine if you had a glass full of black liquid. Consider pouring some out and replacing it with water. The glass is still black but not as black as before. We repeat the process as many times as needed careful to put more water than black liquid. We begin to see through the liquid...something is on the other side. So we repeat and repeat and clearing the liquid until only the water is left. This is the alchemical nature of self-transformation not turning base metals into gold. The goal is for the self to become the gold, the philosopher's stone and know your own inner compass. Knowing this gave me direction.

The Philosophers Stone - The philosopher's stone is a legendary substance, allegedly capable of turning inexpensive metals into gold. It was sometimes believed to be an elixir of life, useful for rejuvenation and possibly for achieving immortality. For a long time, it was the most sought-after goal in Western alchemy. In the view of spiritual alchemy, making the philosopher's stone would bring enlightenment upon the maker and conclude the Great Work. It is also known by several other names, such as 'materia prima.' The Philosopher's Stone, the White Stone by the River, The Sword in the Stone, all the same, meaning that which contains the knowledge of creation, a symbol that represents the final outcome of man's inner transformation, of the conversion of the base metal of his outer character to the golden properties of his higher self. It is all about the evolution of consciousness in the alchemy of time.

Finding the flower of light

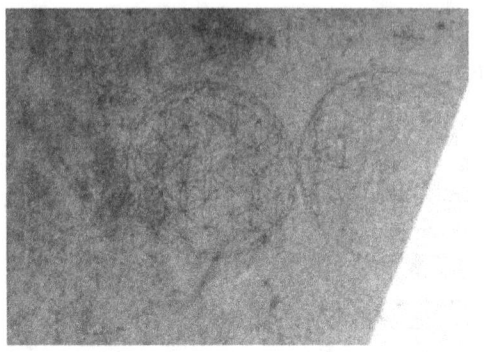

The flower of life is directly quoted in the Emerald tablets referring to it as us, it is the image of infinity like time flowing in its rhythmic motion. TIME – tracking of energy, time is cyclic KNOW THIS – it is NOT LINEAR

"Time changes not but all things change in time, for time is the force that holds events separate. Time is not in motion but ye move through time as your consciousness moves from one event to another" Emerald

I found an image while researching Megalithic Structures from the ancient times (this being from Egypt, however it can be found world-wide). The flower of life is the geometric construct of infamy directly referred to in the emerald tablets. I had seen this image before and I had spent time with the geometry however my knowledge of this flower was zero and my research proved vague at best, even those who claimed to know about it was unable to deliver its meaning in any understandable way. As the months passed the geometry began taking on a totally different meaning which grew aligned with the growing change of perspective created through the many releases leading to that point. At this stage I was involved with the study of cymatics, biology, the occult, frequency, unified field theory, words as spells, religion. The banned books of the bible. Sumerian tablets, the Gnostic texts, the Kabbalah, the Zohar, the Islamic texts and everything I could get my hands on. Bringing together the collective knowledge into one to begin to redefine my minds understanding of the all. My curiosity further extended when in the momentary silence a gateway was unlocked as a portal opened up in my vision as though something had peeled away and I could see something beyond, I couldn't make out what it was and I would've preferred being crazy and call it a day but I wasn't. How did the flower of life and this portal relate to each other? It was as if the clouds had cleared and one could see a sky beyond our sky. I needed to know more, what was I witnessing? This was beyond human. The Egyptians provided the most evidence relating to the flow of consciousness and their megalithic constructions which were built by a different level of comprehension about the inner workings of this earth which is far beyond today's man, thus I turned toward their ancient writings for understanding, specifically focusing on the wheels of consciousness. These earliest wisdoms originated from the Great Mythical Atlantis but unfortunately there wasn't many teachings available aside from the Emerald Tablets. There are older cultures but finding information on them was beyond difficult.

I thought back to my research and I connected the Duat and the virtues of Ma'at which resonated with me deeply as the true journey of life on earth and not the afterlife as the ancients believed. Ironically I had already made this decision to answer the 42 questions along with weighing of the heart vs the feather and the power of living from the heart harmoniously balanced between the heavens and earth and the my path through the time as a child of man amidst the dwellers of old, the children of light and the star beings that from the heavens descended as was reflected in the principles by which the ancients lived. I came to learn of Zep Tepi, "the first time." It was during the First Time or Zep Tepi when gods ruled on Earth the waters of the abyss receded. The primordial darkness was banished and the human biogenetic experiment emerged from the light. The Urshu, a category of lesser divinities whose title meant The Watchers, preserved vivid recollections of the gods themselves, puissant and beautiful beings called the Neteru who lived on Earth with humans in the beginning.

They described the existence of a worldwide pyramid temple system in prehistory mounted like antennae on key energy meridians which were employed by ancient priest-scientists as harmonic tuning forks to stabilize the tectonic plates of the planet's cataclysmic geology. From the mother tongue word Jedaiah meaning "The Way of the Word" or "The

Power of the Word" the ancient Jedai priests used the Language of Light to tune the planet like a giant harmonic bell.

There were 12 areas or major grid points on the planet through which the Zep Tepi moved, creating 12 nations all of which came into being at the same time. Each independent of the other, yet all created by the Zep Tepi who would go by different names in different lands. Some called them the Giants who walked upon the Earth, their exploits recorded on ancient hieroglyphs, sacred monuments and texts as creational myths by all 12 nations each with their own understanding of these creational forces, the Zep Tepi. The bible refers to Giants – *"Genesis 6:4 reads as follows: "There were giants in the earth in those days; and also after that, when the sons of God came in unto the daughters of men, and they bear children to them, the same became mighty men which were of old, men of renown."* My interpretation of this texts and what follows in genesis is based on man's discovery of the energetical abilities of his divinity accessed through the dimensional shift of the divine feminine.

The emerald tablets

I found one of the oldest and most mysterious known writings on this earth The Emerald Tablets created by the Thoth. Known as the master of mysteries, the keeper of records, a mighty Atlantean and Egyptian king. A magician who lived from generation to generation and had passed into the halls of Amenti. He had set down for the guidance of those that are to come after the Emerald Tablets, the records of the mighty wisdom of Great Atlantis. Beginning his incarnation in the great city of KEOR on the island of UNDAL and extending it aeon to aeon renewing his life in the Halls of Amenti where the river of life flows eternally onward. Today its mystery is matched only by the absence of knowing of its actual whereabouts. What interested me immediately was that the tablets were formed through an unknown process which fixes its atomic state, making it indestructible- violating the laws of ionization, breaking our material laws of physics, yet they were created by the hands of man. Who would have such wisdom about laws greater than our own?

It stands to reason that such writings would be of great importance and should not be taken lightly. I wondered why this wasn't public knowledge. You would think that such a discovery would certainly change all that we know. The laws of physics that we base our material world on is broken and we do not know about it? Then again today's world tends toward the intentional suppression of knowledge by the shadow powers who rule so it didn't really surprise me that this was not public knowledge. "Who was Thoth and the Atlanteans I wondered." Through my research I had always thought it was pure mythology and yet now I could access actual material evidence of its existence. I found written translations and audio versions of this emerald tablets and gave it a listen. I also sought to get whatever research material I could find. There is not a lot out there.

Listening to the Tablets for the first time was so strange. This presented a new challenge not because of its complexity and layered codex but I found myself understanding several texts as though I was the one who had written it. Applying my interpretation of the codex within brought results that were verified by later texts in the tablets. There was something here yet again that would put into question the very fabric of what I called reality and in turn change my understanding of it forever. Nothing would ever be the same again for me. Everything I was taught about this world was no longer relevant and forced a complete redefinition and understanding of the true nature of reality even further than the understanding of the hermetic principles. So many of the writings made such sense when the codex was applied. It was weird and yet it put into perspective all that I was experiencing. I could hear things in the tablets that made me feel connected to the unexplainable because what I was experiencing for the most part could not be explained.

I was blown away. At this stage I was spending more time at home. I had begun documenting my experiences using whatever means. I had to, there were things happening in the dark which I would barely remember, these events and thoughts contradicted what I believed, understood and knew. I would write and draw whatever came to mind in the silence for later assessment and understanding. The flower of life began to evolve into different shapes and movements. Drawing presented an opportunity to engage with a different expression of myself. I learnt many things with the flower. Slowly I was creating a comprehendible understanding of its beauty and how its movement worked at its still center thus creating the ever-changing multi-dimensional infinite image of reality and our place in it.

I divided my drawings and aligned my thoughts with them accordingly, linear for left and curve for right, combined for both as one. With the limited information out there relating to the flower I created my own methods which became a valuable tool in accessing areas of the hidden mind especially later on when I came to the knowing that the geometry is not simply geometry. During these sessions I would be very quiet, drawing and listening. Every drawing was me. I would play various types of music and listen to various speakers, sometimes silence. Sometimes ancient Indian flutes, waves crashing, rain storms or healing frequencies. I began to hear the different voices of thoughts more clearly speak in this silent space without thought. It was in the silence that I began to hear myself and only in this silence could the answers be found that are distorted by the noise of everyday living.

The Icosahedron drawn here using the strange angles of the other world to me symbolized the etheric ocean in which the cool fire burns within us all.

With what I learned from inside I began to understand that knowledge by itself meant nothing if it's idle. Like stagnant water becomes toxic. There were times when I became so consumed with the acquisition of new knowledge that I lost sight of my original objective. Knowledge needs to flow through its application to the wisdom it must become creating the knowing required to give birth to true purpose. *"Anyone can say a thing, but can you validate that thing you say?"* I have many times in my life been presented with this situation calling out those who have spoken with empty words. The backlash was that I was labelled as punishing, unforgiving, narcissistic, cruel and unmoving. I've been called a liar, a player on words and twister of fact. I've been told…"you just want to do things your way." I realized that whilst a lot of my truths were harsh they were still true even with the absence of empathy.

I didn't always seek to hurt others as my principle intention. I had judged myself harshly here. I did not appreciate someone saying to me that something cannot be done just because they could not do it. Let's learn together growing by being the willing student instead of a poor teacher. This has always been my principle and I believe it is a worthy principle to live by. In my experiences I've witnessed people abuse their position in favor of the growth learning brings. Strangely we miss the opportunity to grow from what we don't know because we will not admit that we don't, and this stunts our growth. No matter our position or age we can always learn even when it comes from a junior. I had made mistakes, but I was willing to learn. With what was happening to me I had to be sure because it became impossible to speak to anyone about what I was experiencing. I didn't know how to. I always wanted to know as much as I could and strangely at this stage I needed to let go of everything again, I needed to release the power that knowledge had over me.

Chapter 4

Facing the truth

I needed to be less in order to experience truth. I would have to peel away all the layers that had grown thicker through the years, there was so many more than I had thought. Today we say…"That's just who I am." The truth is it isn't who we just are. It's who we've become because of what's collected inside and if some people knew our thoughts they'd not look at us the same. How would we know that this world we call real is not our bondage to the hell created from the beginning of our time, a fractal result of free will's infinite means of expressing itself? I will tell you that Hell and Harmony are only the positions of mind. Why do we kill and oppress in the name of race or religion? Why do we instill fear with our dogmatic doctrine? Love doesn't do that, only the unloved behaves this way. When love is absent we have the age old journey of finding the one thing we don't know we don't use. We won't say it's locked away in pieces because we will not show weakness and be vulnerable. I hear people say all the time…"I won't let anyone make me cry again." We cannot say we use our hearts and speak this way. We don't use our hearts; not enough to end our suffering at least. Not enough to give more than we have taken or live with tolerance and humility. Our fear rules our lives because we have corrupted our purpose, I corrupted mine. I knew I didn't take action leading from the heart. I felt entitled and believed I was above judgment but I was afraid choosing to act from fear pretending I was something I wasn't. I was living a life attempting to achieve a success that I believed would gain me acceptance and respect. I wondered if I was honest for a moment who I would actually be without the armor.

I was the angel and the demon separated because my mind was detached from its many selves. The very things I created to protect me in pain became the monsters I now had to fight working my way free from that pain. This can only be known at the end and not a moment before because I was bound by it, I understood what the voice had told me before and I now knew the mirror would tell me whatever I wanted to hear. It was another difficult pill to swallow because in the beginning the fear creates the most frightful experiences seeing the darkness become real. Seeing the dreams manifest into the real world. Feeling them inside of me and crawling in my skin.

It took me a long time to remember. To learn and know that I was responsible, then to take responsibility and stop making the excuses that I always turned to when things became too much to deal with. I thought I did this before, but I would learn that there are many levels of responsibility. It doesn't help that by design I was born negative into a negative world unaware, unrooted and misaligned existing in the wrong quadrant of expression, yet I chose to be here? This was terribly confusing. I saw this looking through the mirror of illusion as I became more connected with my fragile heart. I never questioned it previously, but I did now and I was beginning to answer the impossible questions with the help of the dweller inside. I was the mirror and the image I had become. I looked through it when I stopped running because I was tired of running from the chaos I created but I had no idea how much was required to take absolute responsibility.

A Quiet mind – Dark heart

Finding the quiet mind in the deeper abyss and being one with this knowing was proving harder than expected. As an artisan working from problem to solution doesn't apply to aspects of the heart when you don't know your own heart or its operations, there is no manual to read for this. So I went to study once more. Not in the classroom. What I sort to learn came from the application of theoretical understanding. My best teachers were the ones who spoke from applied experience not from someone else's experience. I too wasn't above learning, I never assumed I knew it all.

I asked myself many questions again because whilst I still wasn't alive yet for once I was present and sober enough to admit that I wasn't as happy as I could be, and I was still lost in the unsaid and the undone. I never got over my mommy's passing. She died with many unanswered questions and took those answers to her grave. I was so angry for so long, the things I had witnessed. I never spoke of it, I didn't know how to, it destroyed me, and the anger rooted deep like the rotten vines twisting and contracting the life from me. Why was I made to feel so bad for knowing this truth, why could I never make sense of any of it?

Why was it that I had to suffer so badly when I didn't ask to see what I did or know what I knew? The questions I had I couldn't ask, the questions I asked could never be answered. The pain it brought left a madness in the chaos I could never return to rectify. When I asked these questions to others they became what felt like the keepers of the keys of the prison I was locked in. This grew a hatred that seemed to never end. How can you cause a problem then withhold information that could lead to someone else's freedom? I didn't do anything wrong, but I paid a price for it. No one has the right to withhold freedom from another. Knowledge isn't a power to be abused in this way. I was sincere, I just wanted to know why? Why wouldn't anyone ever answer this question, why wasn't I worth an answer. It broke my heart so many times, I'm still suffering, and it still hurts. I struggle to understand why, and I've tried harder than anyone has ever tried to know why these limitations exist?

I don't want to believe that someone would intentionally do something like that. I don't want to consider that someone would be capable of hurting another in this way. I could not understand, and I could not find the courage to ask the questions that had to be asked. I wasn't strong enough to deal with the truth, my hero had fallen, and her warrior had paid the price for his loyalty. After so many years I had lost everything, everything I stood for was a lie. How was I supposed to live with that? She died in silence and I never got to speak to her about what mattered. I was so angry, I lost the last months with her, I lost myself to that anger, I lost myself in those questions and I lost the fight inside of me. I always thought my heart would re-awaken but it never did.

I had repeating problems in my relationships so bad that I even ended my engagement years earlier, it was a difficult lesson to learn. I knew that even though I had released many things there was still many things left inside. What I didn't know at the time is that release without purpose means nothing. Only in purpose can freedom be found and it took a long time to make this connection many times having to relive the same pain over and again. Like the ocean's surface we forget there is a whole world underneath it.

Power from observation

There was one thing I read in my studies that resonated with me repeating in different forms…"Be the observer." I remembered it from before. I continued searching for the key to the silence free from my own interference and observe my frustrations, triggers, pains and sorrows and how it affected my behavior. It's not easy in a world constantly tempting you to engage and when you engage you lose the power of observation and I hated arguing. I grew up in a house where it seemed to be too normal. My parents hurt each other with the unheard hope that something would hit hard enough for a point to be made. It always only served to make things worse rendering a peaceful resolution from which to learn and grow impossible. This cycle repeating, as I grew older I could calculate how and when it would flair up and like clockwork it would happen. I always tried to stay clear of arguing careful never to bring another to tears as I had seen the pain it caused through the years yet I many times I did even when I tried to be reasonable and truthful. I vowed to try and know when I was wrong, but I too found myself lost here. As time wore on, I sought to improve myself at finding solutions that eliminated the need for confrontation. In the end this led to isolation on my part because either I did things alone or somehow an argument would find me. "Why did no one ever speak up?"

I became everything I hated and hated everything I became. I never properly dealt with my frustrations. Instead of reason I would use my presence and aggression when I wasn't heard or found myself being disrespected. Even my good intentions were lost when the person I would engage with was sarcastic in their response, unapologetic in their actions, cruel in their intentions and false in their reason. Have you ever said something so meaningful only to have it met with a sarcastic smile? This is designed to enrage and when you rage the person blames you for being out of control all the while said person is the mastermind of your fury and you are lost in the madness of the moment. There are better ways to deal with these situations than losing control. Only as I grew to know myself better would I learn this. In the beginning I just tried to avoid it all together, this is never the right way. In the end I learned.

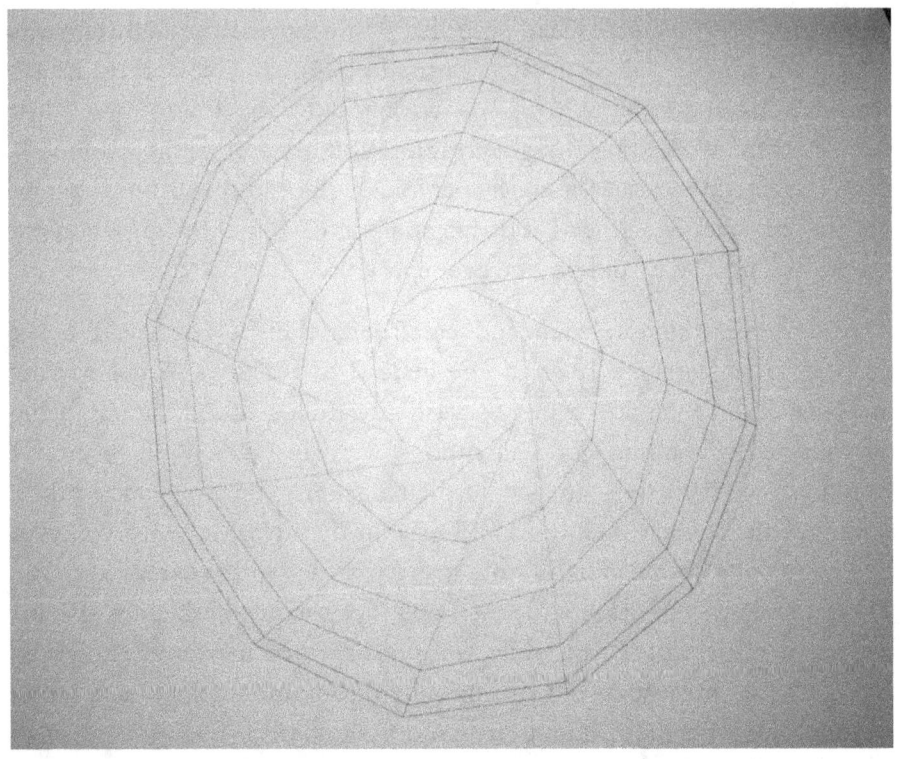

The infinite fractal inward – Look at the geometry and explain why it moves, this is no illusion, consider if all the dimensions were here and now acting out in this world just not as we think. Consider the difference between one radio station and another, if you only knew of one radio station how could you know to tune into another or how to do so. How would you even know to turn the radio on? The key lies in the angles between the lines that move in movements strange to the finite.

I had analyzed and catalogued the collective occurrences when I and others were triggered, the way we all respond and why. It starts with Disassociation which is the involuntary splitting or suppression of mental function from the rest of the personality. It allows expression of forbidden unconscious impulses without any accompanying sense of responsibility for the actions. Our sense of self depends on our feelings – thoughts – sensations – memories – or the perception thereof, if these become disconnected from each other (as a result of trauma).

This was my collective understanding and many times I put this understanding to practice and the results always proved valid. It can be broken down as follows and as per my understanding applying to my mind:

Principle trauma

- Heartbreak – abandonment – rejection
Responses

- Shock denial anger bargaining depression testing acceptance (yes just like the stages of grief)
- We tend to attack first
- Dissociative narcissism
- Worry and anxiety
- Triggering pending severity of trauma (we know them as moods or tempers)
- This is in the low energy realms of 1 (root) and 0 (chaos or rage)
- This temper flairs masks fear and must be managed and sedated with
- Mimicking – to imitate someone in their actions or words
- Unpredictability – quick to change
- Rudeness – a basic lack of manners
- Gas lighting – manipulating someone by psychological means into doubting their own sanity
- Shaming – making someone feel inadequate
- Coveting – secret or hidden intentions

- Poor diet – eats a low vibration diet comprising of fatty foods with little to know interest in bodily health resulting in short bursts of high energy
- Ignorance manages fear – attacking without sense. Defending what you don't understand without common sense or reason. Lying, hoarding, forgetting what you can't process. Selective hearing and poor memory
- You become the very thing you hate
There is another aspect to this

- Trauma creates black spots in our memory, gaps caused by breaks
- Intermittent shutdown or loss of thought and memory
- Causes doubt
- Managed again by anxiety
Gives birth too

- The empathic imposter who is mostly unaware. Struggles with hopeless self-destruction and co-dependence
- Narcissistic imposter who is mostly aware, remorseless and ignorant but weak
Both struggle with doubt

Both are triggered by

- Fear of exposure
- Truth
- Guilt
- Shame
- Pain
- Repeat trauma
- Hate
- Hopelessness
Both uses the same stages which grief uses

- Denial
- Anger
- Bargaining

Depression

Acceptance

One different here is testing

This is managed in the minds filter as I call it. It controls the narrative making changes when needed dumping memory of any triggering information preventing the bridging of gaps, this can be seen as another mirror. Consider those moments when you lose your train of thought or when you are about to say something and you forget everything you were just thinking about. These are no accidents. This happens when you are in risk of raising part of or all the past trauma related to that trigger. You can get these thoughts back if you choose. I got them back with great difficulty and with great physical pain. I will compare it to riding at speed of hitting dead breaks. This is what the mind experiences in those moments. However, to penetrate the darker spaces that is what must be done. I was disconnected and disassociated for a reason and had to remember that. Some of the trauma was so severe that I had created separate entities that became my gatekeepers. To access this space requires an alignment which only I could determine the tolerance of and, whilst you may not require the extreme methods, I used them because it was near to impossible to access some of the darker corners of my mind. In the kabbalah they speak of the abyss in the realms of the higher self, in spirituality they speak of the dark night of the soul. In my opinion it is all the same because we are all the same.

When we can see past fear we can begin to expand in ways that cannot be comprehended when we are bound by fear. To know is to know all of the self. Your ability to create complex geometric images is a direct reflection of the status of your consciousness and the order within.

My Fear

It was the dark corners where the fears dwelled which defined me. I never married, I was always on time, I never had any real commitments, I was always looking over my shoulder, always suspicious. I didn't care unless I absolutely had to and never really apologized for living that way. I was cold, withdrawn and bitter. Addicted to the habits I could never really control. I always thought I could. Fear was aging me and robbing me of any real happiness. I was buried in lies drowning in myself and it was all in my mind. She was right, I had missed so many beautiful moments of my life. We are fed fear daily through the media and other mechanisms creating the mistrust of half facts and altered truths.

Look at the ratio of positive news vs negative news, consider why this ratio exists. The world is not always as bad as is made out to be. I have spent time in war torn countries yet their people are humble, kind and easy to get along with. In fact no different than back home and yet the news will speak of them as radicals, fundamentalists, terrorists, cannibals and savages. I have found in first world countries that people can be equally unhelpful, unkind and difficult to relate to yet the media would suggest otherwise. These lies are perpetuated to feed an agenda that the human population is largely unaware of because they are lost in their own battles.

Withholding information is the essence of tyranny. Controlling the flow of information is the tool used by every dictator in history. As a result of this cycle of fear mongering we send men and women off to war, fighting causes they don't understand, created by people who don't care about peace and in the end logic and reason dies with the rest. Children are blown to pieces and we claim that the sacrifices are worth it for the sake of this false peace. This cruelty can only exist in a narcissistic individualistic, cruel world absent of caring and sharing. If we are meant to love our neighbor how do we justify our actions? There is no flag large enough to cover the shame of killing innocent people. I could see myself in many ways the same as I have described.

"He think that he livith but know it is death within life", While I was living and breathing this was merely the illusion of life by the forces of fear. This was the afterlife, the unknown journey we are all currently taking in this life when we awake we see with the eyes of truth and we know that life was not really life. My initial alignment had evolved in the strangest way. Fear keeps us unknowingly locked away, dead and dying each day over and over only to come back and die again. There is no freedom in fear… *"Fear is the lord of the dark arulu. For he who never faces the dark fear."* This is fear's purpose to isolate us, so we can forget about the whole. The same applies to the inner self and how we have cut ourselves off from it. Many that I've spoken to question my decisions claiming some of what I do is too dangerous based on what they have heard. They are genuine in their concern, yet they make assessments based on unproven facts generated from sources that cannot be verified and yet the fear it generates is real. I have seen areas that have had little to no change in the many years that I have walked and driven but I'm not going to stop walking through them because a news report has labelled them a no-go zone to serve some agenda. I simply reply…"Have you experienced this danger for yourself? What have you based your fear or concern on? Have you sought to validate any of what you are saying?" These are relevant questions that are usually discarded. The fear we show on the outside as caution is the true fear that rules within. Whilst the world is not a bed of roses it is not a warzone either yet news on television says for 97% of a news bulletin that everything is going wrong. I've asked…"What about the things that are going right? What about the good people giving themselves to the benefit of others? What about the acts of kindness that goes unnoticed?" Why are our cameras and equally our minds always focused on the negative? Consider if the news focused on what was

going right with the world and implicating those who are responsible for what is going wrong with the world. Why don't we focus our energies on righting those wrongs? We are the co-creators of this world that we see on the news, the mistrust and suspicion exist, inside of us even those that owns the news and so it manifests into the collective reality. We are responsible for every act of cruelty on this earth, taking responsibility for this however is impossible for most to even consider. We will give it five seconds of thought and then continue consuming whatever the media wants us to consume. Our children are indoctrinated through this same media and parents to easily allow their children exposure to these things because they themselves are not actually interested in the priority of parenting or else they would never allow it. It is easier to put a child in front of the TV or occupy them with a video game than it is to spend quality time with them outside or just as a family doing things families used to do together. I was part of the collective, but I had released a lot of this as the years had passed and I had spoken up against this for many years. For me the remains of this mindset affected me at a much deeper level, I was still a part of this system of control and this had to change.

I decided to redefine our primal fears, this allowed me to transmute a negative to a positive.

- FALLING – descended of source
- LOUD NOISES – notifies us of the vibration and our distance from source
- FIGHT – keeps you in a low vibration away from source
- FLIGHT – rise and fly above your circumstances
- DROWNING – warning of descent into lower denser vibration

Fear made me run away from the truth afraid of what I would find. I knew I may not be able to change everything in a heartbeat, but I could take one step at a time facing my failings in service to the greatest challenge of my humanity. In any war we defend our lives against a destroyer who would devour all, I was my own destroyer. This war was not about the gun and its aggression, the love of a sword and its sharpness, neither an arrow and its swiftness nor the warrior and his need for glory. This was an invisible war and the time had come to make short term sacrifices to achieve long term objectives.

Switch off and reset

I had looked at how I divided my time and realized I needed to do more to enrich my spirit. When we release ourselves from our habits it is easy to get lost in the void of what to replace it with. I was looking for a simpler, better way that would allow me to step out of the dark where I had spent so long. There was more to this world than the sum of my habits and the rippling effects of my choices so I tried to focus on what enriched the spirit, but my raw mind was like an over active child. I needed to coach it into taking the first steps.

I setup a few challenges and worked on a reward-based system so the good and the bad in me would partake in this working together as best as possible, feeding both body and spirit. Simply, if I wanted to ride my bike I had to do some gardening and spend some time listening to anything inspirational and immerse myself in it. I found and used alignment frequencies often specifically the 432Hz and 528Hz, the higher and lower frequencies didn't sound as nice at the time. I would always take a walk to the beachfront. It was weird how calming the serene brutality of the ocean was. It was my favorite thing, sometimes I would stare at it and forget my duties lost in the etheric power I felt with each breath of the salty air. There was always something so beautiful about the way the ocean refuses to stop hugging the shoreline, no matter how many times it was sent away.

The perfection of mind comes from the pursuit of the patience it takes to create a perfect fit for the flower in the construct of the curves of infinity, when the mind is too active 1mm over several replicated circles is several millimetres out at the end potentially in places

I found myself feeling more awake, more at ease and less stressed. I felt myself not having the annoying headaches. I'm no spiritual guru but this worked so I continued and at the same time found myself in the garden barefoot like when I was younger. I spent years in safety boots and protective gear on the oil rigs, ships and heavy industry so taking time barefoot was a wonderful change. Started to get rid of the excess. Turning the soil a bit adding some fresh ground cover and pruning the trees, the dark forest of my mind seemed to be clearing in the light of the morning sun. I had aloe in the garden and found the Egyptians regarded it as a miracle plant so I started using it as they did even moving one inside the house. Quickly my garden was pristine and as nature grows on its own pace I sought to extend the satisfaction into my home taking the task of assessing and organizing all that was inside, applying the same principle as the garden.

When I was younger I was asked to leave the house after my mom passed on. I spent years moving from one place to another many nights unsure where I would be sleeping. It was a difficult time that taught me to find the strength I often didn't have. I carried very little from one place to another so in my home I had what I regarded as only the essentials but when I took stock of everything I realized that I was lying about the essentials. I had way more than I needed without realizing. At a subconscious level I was no different from the extreme hoarders I read about in psychology books. Initially I began to organize myself and my home which whilst kept to a high standard I took extra time cleaning out excess giving away what I didn't need where I could.

In the midst of all of this decluttering I was overwhelmed in an instant of horror as the past and its true pain crept up on me during my cleanup. So much of the past came up once more. I really thought I had made peace with most of these but it wasn't real peace. This time though I felt without any resistance and the pain was unbearable. I thought the unthinkable memories of old and I should've died that day. A thousand years of madness rushed from inside of me. I cried so bitterly. This was far beyond any of those previous releases, like a storm and its destructive path I could only watch myself crumble into the abyss. The hand of the second wave hit harder as more realizations came. The third wave felt as though my heart had skipped multiple beats, it was just like a child who is crying so extensively that their voice disappears. I felt everything. The black hole pulled my eyes into my head with dark rings underneath it. Releasing the pain of it all killed a part of the old me that day as I watched the goose bumps cover my body and face. I didn't know what was happening because I was overwhelmed by the pain. I wasn't going to be hard on myself this time but I didn't know how to help myself either. I was utterly powerless, alone, afraid and lost in desperation. I forgave myself, I found the strength lying on the stairs unable to move to make peace with so much of what I had done and released it from me. I was hurt more deeply than even I had ever realized. There were things I had kept inside through the years of suppression that I watched flow out of me with the tears rolling down my face. *"I fought protecting a reality that cost me my morality and this cycle of insanity is what I called life"* This wasn't life and I was feeling the true agony of misalignment. The true enemy was inside of me, it was me.

Now the day dream had become more real than reality. I was star trekking in the twilight zone unbound by the forests and its mist. It's as if time had stood still and was still standing still. This was the true birth of the observer as I had verified that the incident in the graveyard was not a one-off anomaly. For once I treated myself gently enough to experience the moment even when the moment brought madness. I had accepted that I was to blame and not others. I realized that just because I said I took responsibility didn't mean I had let go of everything deep inside. I knew I had always been fueled by negative but that day it stopped. I made a decision to change that and seek a new way to exist without the negative fuel in favor of a better way of looking at my life. All of the power I used to hurt I would now use too heal.

Painful youth

There were worse pains inside of me. I didn't need anyone to tell me some of these memories never left. This is not how children should grow up and not the example that we should ever learn by. For those who has experienced worse my heart breaks for you. These were terrible times that wounded many of us all so deeply. It breaks my heart to watch the ones I care for suffer because of this. I have wondered about the Law of Free Will and the extent to which it expresses itself and the consequences thereof, the fear it creates will not let go until you let it go. I knew this now. I also knew that my strength had limitations, I wasn't able to face all these dark shadows, the gatekeepers to my freedom. I needed to find the power to stop them and be free. I had no intention of giving in and that was all the strength I needed. Courage is born in this way. Disease is cured in this way. Whenever I found myself down I would remember this statement as it became a shining light on even the darkest day.

Chapter 5

Beyond Human

A gateway had opened inside which I could feel, like wind sweeping over the ocean through the mountains. I could see it on the outside more defined than before, this was a different dimension of existence. I was observing a world beyond the one I knew, it was conscious and moving in order. Why did this happen to me and what was it? I had not been sleeping, I was tired and hungry, keeping myself in a constant state of struggle testing my will. I realized the body and mind was not meant to voluntarily spend time in that state, but I know what I saw, I know how it made me feel. I simulated this state of mind, so it could be controlled to a degree. It wasn't easy, I got frights very easy and badly but despite all of these things I wasn't imagining myself. I could barely describe any of it, but I didn't need to because the feeling was all that mattered.

I stood looking in a mirror speaking to the dweller many times over trying to be as honest with myself as possible. I developed a routine that I would use after I let go. These are some of the words I share with you…"I release myself from the shadows of fear (identify the fear) and shutdown the defenses (identify the defenses) that has kept me safe (identify how it kept you safe) all these years, they are no longer required. I say thank you to the defenses and release them as I am free and no longer need them. I remove any negative energy latched onto me as a result and release myself from this vibration now and forever more"

I had started recording this experience more diligently because the memory loss after the many sessions inside were more extreme than before. I had to will myself to stay there as long as possible recording as much information as I could to use later as my guide but it was different now. I don't have any technical terms to reference this unfortunately. Many times I had to consider if I was entering forbidden spaces because at times it felt that way and there were times when I know I did. I held onto the truthful intent that I was working on improving myself to become a better person free of all the filth, the confusion of never knowing and always repeating ending at the same place I began over and over again. These spaces and my growth was directly aligned with the truth. Honesty kept me holding on and moving further inward but I wasn't always honest, in the end I paid for the absence of that honesty many times over.

A degree of reason

From a human perspective I had to create some understanding of this because the conscious mind was having some issues experiencing things that at times appeared unreal. I was lost in mystical nature of it all and felt like I was back in the dark forest, I didn't even know to imagine these things so simply this became another Master Reference. "I don't know to imagine what was happening." I realized if I could not imagine it I could not fake myself into believing it was happening. With this in mind I tried to find anything out there that could aid my understanding. The closest I got was "the third eye" and I had no idea what the third eye was aside from my research but I was led to believe that the pineal gland had atrophied over the generations for all humans and was inactive, I had never met anyone who could describe what I was experiencing. I wasn't looking in the right place once more, I had to expand my search.

More research was required getting as much information as I could from the most unlikely sources. I read the Bible, the Quran, the Kabballah, the Zohar, and the Eastern ancient teachings. I found in the Bible the book of *Matthew* reads... *"When the eye is single thy whole body will be full of light"* other religions and cultures spoke of it too. The ancients lived by it. Hindu culture speaks of how to experience it. Asian culture teaches how to use it via Chi, modern spirituality explains how to access it. In fact, modern spirituality provided the most information relating to this matter along with the Hindu culture and Reiki. I found symmetry between the piezoelectric effect in crystals and its relation to the pineal gland. This helped me make sense of the colors I was seeing. The tablets spoke about this however all other research I had done spoke of the intuitive visualization of and not actually seeing and witnessing the experience. This made me question whether there was more to the connection between the inner and outer world than anyone understood. I remembered the Hermetic Principle as above so below. The Nacaals from pre-history and Egyptians knew about this and it aligned with divine law. Is this what they meant?

Something interesting started happening when I closed my eyes. I was seeing a purple haze pulsing like a beating heart then spiraling into the black space like you would like the gases of galaxies spirals. The red and orange/yellow blotches were gone. Before I never questioned it and never bothered with it because I figured that's just the way it was and there's no information to aid further understanding, at least none that I found. Now I had to wonder about this space inside. This once dark space was now active and moving in order. The purple pulsing spiral occurred around rest time either lying down or bed time round about the time I fell asleep. There was a slight pulling effect like I was being nudged into another space, another world. It was very weird and equally beautiful. I tried once more to speak about what I was experiencing but I was ridiculed again. Even family whom I shared most of my life's story with was particularly critical and I found it strange. This took its toll on me. Only later I would fully understand the nature of reflective reality, at this point I was so hurt that I did not know how to deal with the backlash.

I turned inward for answers but sadly during this time I lost a child. I didn't want to lose the child, but the choice was taken away from me. I wish I had fought harder, I should've but I didn't. It hit me so hard and forced me to look deeper for reasons and understanding as to the universes plan. I tried to distract myself hoping to see a positive lesson through this difficult time rather than respond to the anger and grief inside. No one knew of the child or my suffering and I never told anyone. I paid a high price and a part of me wanted revenge, a part of me took revenge. The old way had crept in and I wanted someone to suffer as I was but I was done with that way, I thought I was done with that way. Even still I should've done more but I didn't and that in itself was revenge. I was consumed by regret and the pain compounded what felt like new chains binding me to the old way. It was tough dealing with the grief, I often questioned whether I wasn't creating the experiences after as a result of the grief. I had to be honest about everything and analyze all eventualities even if I didn't like the answers. I did not appreciate the truth of this moment but that didn't make the truth less truthful. My heart was breaking, I had just started putting it back together and now this dark sadness had taken my smile. I could feel the grip of the spirit of vengeance and its unwillingness to let go, I could feel it crawling inside, a chaos of rage tearing away wanting to be unleashed. I began to understand the Mirrors power that lay between above and below. This was one of the hardest lessons I've ever learnt feeling this cruelty with my open heart bleeding in my hands made me realize how fragile the heart truly is.

"Through order ye shall find the way. So ye that the word came from chaos? Saw ye not that light comes from Fire? Look in thy life for this order, balance and order thy life. Quell all the chaos of the

emotions and though shalt have order in life. Order brought forth from the chaos will bring thee the word of the source."

Begin to understand

I was down and been tortured by some of my history, this was all too familiar. I had a choice to make, the hardest one I have ever made. A part of me wanted to set the madness free and watch everything burn to the ground. I wanted to destroy it all and rain down an ungodly suffering on everyone, but I couldn't. Something was different, something had changed. I didn't want another to suffer the way I was suffering. No one should ever feel this way. I couldn't do it anymore, I just couldn't bring myself to unleash hell. It wasn't worth it, not anymore. Instead, I cooled that negative directed toward me and transmuted it into a positive as best as I could. I started being politer and tried smiling more. I took some time to be a light to myself and those around me. I stopped running and started walking, often breaking down along the road, it didn't matter anymore if anyone saw me. I parked my bike and started using public transport. I started observing the sky in a new silence. I began to test my limitations going deeper into the ocean each time, alone with the wind and the waves of time cooling down that fire of vengeance. Through it all I began to enjoy caring for myself and taking the time to do so looking after my feet, hands and face. I shaved my hair and eased up on the self-torture. I became more active in remembering to be kind and patient with myself and others through all the bad that had happened. I was learning to a degree the power of respect and living just a bit lighter despite grieving the loss. I was smiling just enough that it made me feel better.

I found the courage to write apologies to many people I had wronged along the way breaking down terribly remembering all that I had done. I even apologized for my part in the pregnancy and loss with no expectation of replies because I had reached a point in my life where I was man enough to admit that I was wrong. Though it had been many years for some the least I could do was take responsibility for the things I know I had done wrong. I even found the strength to release those who hurt me that I took revenge on apologizing for that revenge. I could see how I had become everything I said I wouldn't and it broke me again so severely as I was aligned with the pain I had caused others and they had caused me. I was so sorry for the so many of the things I had done. There were no excuses, I was guilty. I was a monster, the blackest of the shadows reflected in the mirror and I struggled to face it. It was time to know the demon in me. Going back into the past I knew I could've done many things differently but I didn't. Sometimes I celebrated others' demises and ridiculed them so it was right that I was suffering. I was paying for all I had done. I was guilty and the shame consumed me. This pain was too much to bear. These are not easy things to come to terms with. When I saw my reflection in the mirror it changed me yet again. From the obvious confusion of not fully understanding what was going on again a part of me knew what was inside. There were two who witnessed what happened in the mirror. I saw their reactions and they saw mine, that's how I knew this was all real. It was time to raise more. I knew I had to go back down yet up into that dark space even though I didn't want to. I wasn't done yet, there was more I could feel it, much more and I knew I was still missing parts of me.

When we fractal back to the fire we begin to see the circle of origins, then we can begin to understand that the fire must be cooled to give birth to the true fire. "Should you will to know who lies beneath sit in front of a mirror and look into it without blinking. Do not blink for as long as you can. Your eyes will burn but you must resist blinking. All will be revealed if you can manage not to blink and still your mind as you cycle through your energies they will be revealed to you."

But I was still struggling to find the stillness I needed to explore the equilibrium within the zero point. I wasn't lost but in this moment, I didn't know where I was exactly and these are times one can open the wrong doorways when one's mind is jaded between here and somewhere. I had an issue with the idea of being manipulated by unseen forces so consequently I released myself from the good and bad not knowing the difference between the two because I didn't know myself well enough to determine that difference. *The Emerald Tablets read…"Discourse with the ignorant as well as the wise"* I didn't do it aligned with the tablets, I was just fed up.

With all the confusion and pain I knew deep down I had found something worth fighting. I would find myself again no matter the odds. The ups and the downs were crushing at times, but I wasn't defeated yet, not as I once was long ago. This is part of unwinding, it isn't what I wanted to hear but it is part of the impossible challenge of finding infinities heart. Love and pain and that circle of opposites yet always same. I was beginning to feel like true love can only exist as a shadow, a loyal companion that never leaves- always there, watching yet we never notice. Steadfast and just between the angles, knowing us in our light and dark moments, changing forever just as we do. I had found hope and hopelessness in the unthinkable spaces between the worlds of light and dark. I wondered about the purpose of purpose. I wondered many things during this time. I remembered what the voice said long ago, that we never take enough time to appreciate the thorns on a rose rather we complain that it hurts us. I wondered whether I should be more grateful not that because of the Rose tree has thorns but rather that a Thorn tree has roses.

I grew from these cryptic lessons presented even when what I was trying to show myself didn't come through positive means I began to understand why. Were it not for the thorns I would forget to be gentle with the rose. Many times, I had to get hurt because I ignored what the universe was trying to tell me so the message had to be brought more aggressively until I got it. All these are coded in reverse. Synchronicities of alpha numeric codex gifted by the universe that I many times openly ignored. Repeating numbers, words, times, moments, faces, songs, dates were all designed to show me the unlearnt lessons within. I had asked the question then ignored the inconvenient answers so again I was right where I was supposed to be.

I turned to writing once more. A proven mechanism for me to open my heart. I would flow as the music whispered reminders of the words I was unable to speak. This helped so much and took my mind into an expressive silence drawing on the force of my wounded heart. I would burn the pages. Sometimes I couldn't, sometimes I didn't want to burn them. This made me enquire deeper to gain more understanding about rooted issues I wasn't fully aware of. I had been to the darkness more times than I could remember and more times still bridging gaps of the pathways inside but there was more still, we can never be aware until we are aware, and I was aware that there was more pain to come. This alignment though brought me closer to the infinite wave like those moments when you see something out of the corner of your eye and you are so sure you saw something, yet you still wonder if you did. I may not have understood exactly what was happening but I could see new colors growing in my reflection. I noted changes in the colors, its order and definition when my thoughts and actions changed. I got more involved eating a "coded" diet. All fruit and veg that have the sacred geometric code in its shape. I aligned the colors of the food with the chakras using the seven days of the week making Thursday day 4, chakra 4 etc. I used traditional root and spice detox drinks which tasted bad in the beginning. I wore colors orientated around the specific chakra for the specific day using that day to focus on that energy meridian.

Before I could experience love's beauty I had to deal with love's pain but the extreme nature of these releases and changes were taking its toll on me. The split of two selves was too much still trying to balance the old and the new in the outer world. At times it felt like the harder I pushed toward unity the harder I pushed back. I should've made the transition but I was resisting, still holding onto fragments of the old way. There was a moment in the madness I sought to kill the ego in me, I was so frustrated that I had caused myself all this hardship I wanted to remove what I believed was the cause of my suffering. When you research the ego in today's society we are told of the false self. I was angry because again I was still looking at everything in separation, not realizing it was all me. I wanted everything out of me, absolutely everything had to go. A clean wipe. Amazingly a voice said with such sadness…"Why are you trying to kill me, I have always been there for you. Since the beginning keeping you safe when you were not able to face the pain I was there looking after you making sure no one hurt you, I don't deserve to die."

Sitting down that day waiting between somewhere and nowhere I burst into tears realizing that I was again willing to kill without thinking. I wasn't willing to take a moment to consider, no patience within to allow myself to see what was right in front of me. I created all of me even the ego. I was responsible. Who was the real monster inside of me? It felt that every part of me was rotten, yet I was doing my best to improve. Why then is all this horror cycling round and round again? I was trapped in my own inability to make good lasting choices in favor of the convenient ones that brought quick reliefs but whose prices I'd always pay later never thinking of the price in the moment.

Everything in me was tainted by my perceptions and contradictions. The more I was releasing the more came to the surface. Some things I didn't want to face without even realizing. I was lying to myself again to avoid the absolute reality as even for me it was too much. Whilst I said I was smiling more often I found myself miserable after. I had lost my smile again just as I had found it. My horrible dreams killing me every day and it got worse as time cycled on. I was in so much pain again. How did I end up back here so soon? There were some triggers hidden so deep I couldn't tell that I was still trapped in old cycles of mine. I was so sad everything hurt, and I couldn't stop crying. I couldn't stop feeling every part of my 37 years was ripping me to pieces like I was right back at the beginning again. Even though I felt better the pain of the past was so severe I was struggling to see any purpose or end to this madness. Each time I would go inside the cycle would repeat with moments of beauty and moments of agony. It felt like a never-ending battle trying not to let the light go out never fully realizing THAT I WAS THE LIGHT.

Even the monster in me was broken too. Everything was broken, nothing was right and again nothing was worth fighting for anymore. I had no fingers left to point. All I could feel was the never-ending sorrow. I was standing in the mirror looking at another black figure in front of me. There was compassion even for the blackness in me because there was nothing left. I had equally held onto the hurt and the hate as everything else at a deeper level that I had not penetrated before.

It was in this madness that I found a light reflected as shadows of fire. It appeared as three in what can be described as reflecting light distorting my vision that took the shape of me along with a similar image of a female who appeared to be crying and facing the other way. At this point I had grown tired of the fear, I had enough of being stuck in the mud step after step. That day I stood my ground and said "no more" as they flew toward me it felt as though they became one with me and the moment passed. One of them was still there. I tried to communicate with her but she seemed too emotional to speak and a while later she disappeared. I would find this experience in the Tablets. *"Few there are who has looked on the mighty face and lived, for not are sons of men, are The Children of Light when they are not incarnate in a physical body"*

That day I took a moment with all the broken pieces of the different minds that still dwelled within and all unilaterally committed to self-improvement. It was time to merge into one whole to become what I was always meant to be. I screamed inside "I can feel everything. I am not afraid to feel anymore." I was finally willing to express my true feelings free as I once did. There was a better way than this and I could become one with all of me. I didn't have to be a monster anymore. I was the light and it is inside of me. The chaos and the order.

I wasn't the bad person I had made myself out to be and I was going to get this right. I was going to break the cycles that were still repeating. I was stronger than this, I knew I was but I needed a new plan. The original methods required evolving because I was evolving. I theorized using the flower of 19circles all disorganized that I could remove 1 circle at a time until there was no more circles instead of removing all of them at once. I could then draw the first and create a shape worth looking at. The pain was just too much to remove it all at once even though I knew I wouldn't show myself more than I could manage but I went too far. I had to admit that some of my methods were wrong and thus my focus shifted to finding the courage and discipline to implement lasting change with patience at my center. I became more organized in my approach to allow myself to affect this lasting change I was lacking in the current chaos I was experiencing. It was time to take flight and rise into a new way. This was the order that time and the light brought from the chaos of night.

- Self-enquiry
- Intermittent fasting (gateway)
- Observation
- Define your master reference
- Question
- Know the truth from the lie
- Be honest (gateway)
- Challenge
- Do not accept narrative
- Let go (gateway)
- Forgive (gateway)

- Shutdown the defenses at zero point (gateway)
- Hold my new vibration 21 – 90days
- Keep my heart open (gateway)
- Flow with moments of beauty
- Learn to show love (gateway)
- Give more than I have taken
- Reset and rebirth a new fractal version
- Document old vs new
- Do this again and again till all one becomes one
- Define new rules and honor it
- New routines and stick to it
- Be kind to myself
- Keep smiling (gateway)
- Give smiles to others (gateway)

Habits, energy and order

It was no accident that in my observation I saw moments of beauty that didn't last. I had no understanding of the flow of energy even less about what exactly was happening as there is nothing to reference it against. When I returned from my momentary created vibration to my default vibration it was because of my unconscious position. It's designed this way. In modern times we speak of cognitive dissonance, a mental discomfort experienced by a person who simultaneously holds two or more conflicting or contradictory beliefs, ideas and values. This discomfort was triggered when my belief clashed with new evidence perceived by me. My mind retreated and reset to a place of safety before the trigger. From the original theory to the many applications I understood this now. Think about when you run, your heart rate goes up, when you stop it comes back down again. Consciousness works in exactly the same way, it always sounds simple after but the pain won't let you see that. I always found myself pulling toward material relief which I had to stop if I wanted to continue inward. I was been torn from one extreme to the other with no rest position of reference.

So I created another effective Master Reference. Anything that made me want to do anything that potentially harmed the body and spirit was bad and had to be noted. This may sound obvious but when you are torn between an unknown known and an unknown unknown we tend toward what we are familiar with not realizing the implications as we are still in part disassociated to the fact. I didn't have to give up the bad per say simply be aware when such behavior occurred and why. I would point a finger at myself and asked the question…" Why am I making this decision?" This became a very effective way of creating constant awareness. Thus I began tracking the voices and its energy, understanding the issue and resolving it slowly yet ever surely merging one with the other in my attempt to create a whole. The hardest thing to do was ordering and understanding the varying energies and its desires. Understanding that trauma was separated by the varying energies and alternate sides of the myself meant the many selves had to be individually dealt with as separate yet part of the whole. One-self, one brain – two sides – two selves equally polarized – four hearts – seven energies equally polarized. There were many that dwelled within and this is only the example of using the seven system. At least this is what I had determined through my experience.

The tree of knowledge in the kabbalah is of good help here, I didn't overcomplicate things by trying to decipher the doctrine in its complex nature. Instead I made it simple, the balance comes from the order true flow creates in the same way all of light has different frequencies. I looked at the tree as several spinning wheels that had to be individually brought to the correct spinning frequency according to the divine order by converting the knowledge to wisdom through release, understanding and ordering aligned with the law and that was the key. This is a process that one takes with the clues presented in the outer world. One by one I worked my way through myself as busy and distracted as I was at times. This can be an impossible place to find order when all that exists there is still the chaos from the beginning. I used the process of alchemical transmutation, *(banish -release - let go – reset – shut down defenses - do again)* as many times as was required until the silence becomes easier to locate within.

Ritualizing the experiences and creating a consistent routine was the most effective way. I used whatever made me feel comfortable, always looking at myself in the mirror and, though this wasn't needed, I do suggest it is used. I generally started going inward from late afternoon till mid-morning incorporating sunset and sunrise. In doing so I had access to both night and day to partake in the varying energies either offered. Also night time is quieter so it provides the means to enjoy outer silence whilst searching for the inner silence. I would drastically reduce eating, drinking and sleeping on Thursday till Sunday. I kept the house very cold opening all the windows during night time and keeping the lights dim and when possible not using the lights at all. This heightens the sensors and allowed me to activate other areas of the mind. The key is the switching, it can be felt. It is a strange feeling as if you are not really here and yet you are.

As time went by I wasn't as severe with myself because it wasn't needed anymore. If you wish you and your partner can do this together without the mirror. You and a friend perhaps or you and your child. Being honest and speaking from the heart may be near to impossible for some. It may be impossible to tell a husband the child is not his or for a husband to tell his wife that he had an affair with a member from your mosque. Grow together or grow part, either way you make your choice. I'll say this…"if you struggle with high blood pressure and you are keeping secrets the medication may help treat the symptoms but releasing the secrets will cure the condition."

The secret is discipline when working through the human disposition as one begins to see the power of free will and the grip of the manifested consequences of sin. I struggled to maintain my discipline initially with my affirmations, diet, and fasting, I really struggled with the fasting. Obeying my exercise routine and my total change of lifestyle and mindset. I even struggled at times with the writing and I really missed riding my bike. It took its toll trying to obey my heart's requests over my body's desire and remain positive through the detoxification periods which at times was a nightmare then still continuing long after with the changes and the initial growth. Finding the strength to face each day discharging myself from the many parasites within that were holding on tighter and tighter as I released more of myself. Staying true to the objective without succumbing to my own misleading nature attempting to return to the safety of the now distant old way in favor of the abyss of the unknown where my stomach groaned as the hounds came closer with every shift of my mood. I found myself alone in tears more often than the joy of the sedation a drink or fast meal brings. Later on as progress was made the same sedatives were no longer effective and this is really difficult because now there is no old way to return to and no new way to see yet. This is especially challenging and will test one's will to the limits often bringing thoughts of regret because now I really didn't know the difference between who I was and was not.

Chapter 6

A new look at the old way

We often say we regret nothing, this is fair but the truth is everyone regrets something. I found myself again reflecting on the past knowing that I had not completely let go yet because some things mattered so much to me that I was looking for a specific closure. This was a mistake and I learnt from it tackling the history of my parents. Having to make peace with the truth that I had ignored growing up would prove one of the most influential aspects of my growth. My mommy was not the angel I made her out to be and my father whom I hated for so long and blamed for so much was not the devil I made him out to be. This was a hard step but an important one, it was time and it's been a long time coming. It was a dark blind spot over my life and I was ready to remove it. To face the enemy and the mirror.

This holds the key to the gateway through the next dimension of consciousness, its secrets lie in the angles used to create the image itself, known in the tablets as the strange angles it must spin for you to cross.

My parents despite the history did attempt to instill values that today makes sense yet yesterday were lost in the emotional chaos of the moment. Many lessons fell on deaf ears with the hatred that grew inside and I blocked it all out. It was easy to just ignore than to have to deal with some of the things that happened along the way. One cannot always blame a child for this, although as some children grow they can become manipulators and use the parent's guilt for personal gain this is a secondary effect of the principal problem and I was never interested in doing that. Parents pay the price by being shown their true hidden nature reflected in the children they create. The children becomes the unlearnt lesson and many times parents say…."I've got no idea why this child is this way" Children reflects the inner you. Their restless minds are a reflection of your restless mind though no parent wants to admit that they are at fault. Children suppress what they don't understand and feed this suppression, not knowing the origins no different from the parents. They feel shamed and guilty never knowing that their unusual attraction to women is because their father who they idolize was and still is a womanizer and the mother ignores it because she married for money and had children to secure their relationship. Men, your children doubt themselves because they look to you as the hero who can do all things but you never tell them you are only able to do a fraction of the things you claim because you speak more than we act. When children fail they feel as though they have failed you not realizing you have failed yourself. They feel ashamed that they cannot live up to your standards when in fact your standards are far lower than you let on. As they grow older they begin so see the holes in the stories you tell. At some point they choose to expose you and grow into a better person yet even though they are right and you have the opportunity to set them free you defend your failings and make them doubt themselves. This is fundamentally wrong and should never be allowed to happen. As elders we are the keepers of the wisdom. What wisdom are we really passing on? If we as elders advise the next generation to follow a better path why should they when we ourselves do not follow the very path we are instructing them to follow. How do we expect anyone to listen to us?

I was still angry and hurt because these issues are still relevant today and I have been advocating this most of my life. It is not okay to live above the example. As children we only knew that we are repeating the lessons of the previous generation fighting the same wars thinking it is our own we could break the cycle. When we seek advice we go to the very people that have hurt us and withhold the truth from us. trapping us in the very cycle we believe is unique to us. They don't tell us they themselves are guilty and so they cannot give advice but they do in bias, molding and shaping the advice around their guilt and the shame corrupts the advice, so we the children are lost from the start. We have been doing this for all ages. We live separated from ourselves and the effects of our choices. We know we are wrong but we defend the filth that dwells inside, pretending to be everything we envy. The lie that becomes our lives thus must be protected to our deaths, never to be revealed and this is how our poles shift into the triple negative, this is what kills us in the end.

As I thought about all of these things a deeper anger raised new shadows. I was so angry at myself, my parents, my teachers and at people in general for all the lies and rubbish I had put up with. Why couldn't people just say "I DON'T KNOW" instead it is always something, an excuse, a story that I as a young person and even as an adult would naively take the word as truth...."Why would someone lie?" I've asked myself this so many times. I had come to understand the reasons yet still it disturbed me because it hurt to think that was all I was worth. It was never right and it will never be right. It's heartbreaking to know the ones I looked up to had many times lied to me and in turn I've used those lies to build my life on. This was the sad nature of things. What I learnt though is how we treat that lie defines our character. It bent mine and I broke many times before I learnt what I know now. How do you find the goodness in such tragedy? I wondered back to the spirit of vengeance for just a moment but I was observing with an open heart and learning to forgive because I now knew that the power of fear can grip even my heroes. I began to see the dweller and not just the shadow. I realized that most of my once heroes are themselves still lost in the wilderness of the unknown.

That day I released something. I didn't know what it was or how to describe it. It was such a powerful experience watching a black shadow leave me and leave the house. One of the many selves fractured into existence by my life's choices. It was me, a part of my many creations. That day I realized harmony is knowing the good and the bad, not ignoring one over the other. That day I stood in the great wall as the guardians grew beside me. I was so afraid watching the shadow outside the window as it waited for my thoughts to return so that it too could return. I realized I cannot leave a space I don't know I'm trapped in, I simply wouldn't know to leave. I was bound by that unknown trigger and when triggered I missed the lesson but I was breaking free. I was starting to comprehend at a level far beyond my original perspectives.

"There are tipping points where we drop into zero and the chaos of rage. These triggers unleashes responses that at times appear beyond human control for the human is shutdown in these spaces. The actions and words comes from a gatekeeper inside and will destroy anything and everything until the threat is removed." Despite this I had to admit that even in that automated darkness I was still conscious even when I had little to no memory, I could still choose to see the truth of what's happening instead of allowing the moment to consume me and thus the outcome because these actions came from a place that I created. But I cannot compare myself to everyone. Sometimes good people who suppress the inner madness can succumb to it in fits of rage and the result is catastrophic. Unfortunately once we return to cognition we cannot understand why we allowed ourselves to go that far with the malicious actions taken. I'm not defending anyone who hurts another. No woman or man deserves to experience this. However and I say this very carefully, there are some people who are aware of the advantage they can gain in a relationship and know exactly how and when to trigger

their partner. The regret destroys our humanity. This same delusion applies to many examples. Weak people who use Gas lighting to destroy their partner's self-worth in the end making themselves and others believe they are insane. This is a cruel thing to do. Even in these circumstances though the partner has a choice and can leave. *"If you stay it is because you choose to stay and you will have to ask the question why you stayed."* We cannot make excuses or project blame for what happens. We cannot abuse others' sympathies when we are the cause of our own problem. We cannot take others energy when we knew what we were doing. We were aware of the potential harm and we did it anyway. We cannot even blame the partner because we are equally guilty. I would rather be homeless than be rich, miserable and tortured. I would rather leave and learn from the experience than stay and hurt a woman I claimed to love, this will never be love. This is simply weakness and comes from a bad place.

Even more subtle is intimidation, the product of jealousy grown from insecurity and the paranoia it creates. This too is not love. There is no such thing as being overprotective, that's nonsense. If your relationship requires you have a password on your phone or call your partner continuously there is a serious problem. What do you need privacy for when a relationship is defined by love? What kind of love requires privacy? Why do you need to check your partner's phone to begin with? When did love require boy's nights out? Why do we need to run? What are we running from? What are we hiding? What is really going on in the minds of people? This is proof of deep rooted issues in the modern person. It makes no sense and yet today it is exactly how things works and accepted as normal.

This is disturbing and yet when I have raise this subject in a company I am made to feel as if there is something wrong with me because either "I single you don't get it" or "when I am a parent I'll understand" or "I not married I can never understand" the same excuses are used to deflect from the cold hard reality of our true intentions and the inner mind that dwells in the dark corners of what religion calls the devil's temptation. It's not the devil. Don't blame the devil when we are the devil.

Look at your parents as I did, who they are today was not who they were before you were born. Look at your life today as I did and see the relationships as they are a reflection of the past. Coming to know this brought a lot of peace for me because we don't know the whole story. Not all people are bad but men do cheat and so do woman just like lying and it's a reality. No one is above the negative and no one wants to imagine calling granny a whore yet that's why grandpa is an alcoholic because grandma cheated on him four times in their marriage while he was working away or Mommy is a staunch Jew whose god is everything to her because Daddy had a child with her best friend when she was pregnant and they had just got married. She chose to stay because he was hers? The same applies to single parents who uses children as weapons because they are bitter and angry at the partner. Even before they are born they are used as a means to an end, I know I have experienced this first hand and it breaks a person. Children are raised hearing how terrible their father or mother is being called nasty names, the children never knowing the truth of the history and the parents never telling the truth of that history. They change the history into whatever truth is required to rationalize the things they know they have done. These are the things we do to each other in the name of love. We have no right to do these terrible things and yet this is how we use our free will.

In many cases fractals will break off and new fractals will begin. A consequence of the polarization and de-polarization effect. Two negatives create a positive etc. People don't know this. That's why some children's mannerisms are the complete opposite of their parents, depending on the sum of the previous generations actions will determine the change in the fractal that is the children they create. They want nothing to do with the business of power and rebel. This is designed to show the parents how they have ignored aspects of their selves in favor of the power. In my observations these truths became difficult to ignore and taught me many important lessons.

As we grow through the experience of peeling away the many selves we must know when to vocalize and when to observe. To use our emotions as a tool for new life and not as a tool to take life away. This image has the flower of life overlaid on the construct inner first flower. It allows one to see the proportions of infinity vs the finite this can manifest as the female egg in humans.

The power of emotions

"Searched I infinities heart through all the ages, deeper and yet deeper, more mysteries I found" Emerald Tablets. For most it may seem pointless to relive the emotions inside yet they define all that we are. What we suppress is slowly killing us. What we give birth to reflects that suppression, every action and its seemingly random reaction.

This imbalance was the cancer inside of me slowly spreading and infecting all of me. When I considered the technical definition for cancer it allows me to see and know this…"For *unknown reasons the cells starts to move opposite to the general movement of cells in the body."* It isn't unknown. When we search within we know the things that we have done which we ignore, that is why the pain hurts so bad. The choices we have made that has caused us as a whole to first look the other way then to flow the other way all together. When we accept what we know isn't right and make it our truth our poles shift. In this new space if we lose one of our poles the result manifested is the reverse cellular movement that becomes the cancer we know. Cancer is a symptom of the change inside and is thus the cure as it reveals the disposition of the mind and the true direction of the inner self. When we understand this we can find solutions, when we find our true balance. Reinstating the poles and rebalancing them, working through the mind and heart using mechanisms like vibrational and nutritional therapy after we have released the imbalance within. Releasing myself from my own imbalances and aligning myself with the law paved the way for the improvements with my own illnesses. Where previously I would get sick every change of weather and simply being close to someone who was sick made me sick - now I rarely if ever get ill. I've not used an asthma pump for a very long time when previously I was using it six to eight times per day. I use zero medication of any kind where before I was addicted to antihistamines painkillers, vitamins etc.

My new applied formula was working and I started to feel like I could do this. Letting things go properly that had returned and consumed me became easier. I began to notice goodness not just the bad. I found myself waking up earlier, spending more time outside. Losing weight as my diet naturally improved. I was greeting strangers and helping others more. This time it felt different, empathy was growing inside of me. A new sense of compassion I had never known. I was learning to live from the heart and I was growing in line with the law and it really made me feel so good. The influence was so strong that I was going to make some big decisions which ordinarily I would not even have considered. Some lessons that needed to be learnt required removing any comforts that potentially still blinded me that without these decisions I'd not have learnt of what was deep inside, beyond my knowing.

I went back to the end again this time with a more open perspective and asked the same questions once more…"What was driving me? What fears still restricted me? What are my tolerance levels and how patient was I really?" You see sometimes we can be too nice, too patient and too tolerant. Sometimes our failing is being an enabler, this was an important lesson. Sometimes the journey through this space and time is to learn to be less tolerant and less enabling. To know the difference between compassion and enablement. Goodness emerges from the balance of knowing both sides of the circle and not just the one side, thatis the true nature of cyclic energy and not linear ascension. Letting go of the anger brought a force that took me the deepest I had ever gone inside….

"Wounded soul rest now for you are healing. The pain you feel is but seasons passing for the last time. Your shattered dreams and broken heart serves a greater purpose that has led you here. You are not blind anymore, these are no longer the eyes you remember. See the light and the eye within. Know the effect of your cause. See your soul as it grows from the night that surrounds you. Great warrior your troubles are not in vein. Your tears have been wiped away with the spirit of life. Time may have divided us but you are beyond time, you may be filled with questions and recriminations and guilt but that's only part of love, that's part of being human. These are the fragile moments that make life worth living."

"Rest your weary head on my shoulder and I will not let go. We are all so proud of you. We didn't think you would make it this far, no one has made it here for a very long time. Let your tears flow. The war is over and you can rest now, your fight is done. A new journey is beginning. Look inward and be one with the fire, know that you were never human. Take time and see the truth of this world. Look everywhere and you will find the same for all is your own. Where you are is where you are meant to be. All the wisdom you seek lay within. To find the wisdom you must continue to give and let go till all ones become one in one purpose. Then you will walk hand in hand with the Lord of the world. Fear not, have the courage to follow your heart wherever it goes. You are creating the steps you take now. You have awoken from the death you know as life. " Remember these words of Power…"I am the Light, in Me is no Darkness"

She was the voice of my heart, ever calm vibrating softly, a dream I never wanted to wake from, a walk in the shadows far from this world where soul's burn in the fire of love's eternal light. She was a reminder of what I was, a reason worth not waking up for and every time we spoke I never wanted to. I wanted to stay there with her forever. That would've been enough for me, lost in the wilderness with her at my side dancing in the moonlight where time exists not, this beautiful enigma. There is no other form of communication more powerful than the loving hand of infinite calm. That's how she made me feel. A compassionate touch of her hand and reassuring hug took away my fears. It filled the emptiness with the spirit of love.

The equilibrium born of a new expression of yourself

As I was growing up I missed the hugs. My dad and I never really was close enough to share many. I remember holding my mommy as she took her dying breathes in this life, succumbing to cancer's cold grip. I remember when my two best friends whom I spent most my life growing up with died suddenly soon after my mom. My dad put his hand on my shoulder and that meant so much. Whilst this encounter took place when I was alone, within, the voice and its silent whispers was the most needed hug I had ever received in my life. The most comforting I could remember and badly needed as at times I wanted to give in to the hopelessness I often felt. I restored hope again allowing myself to feel the warmth of love and experience the truth that had made me shutdown many times over. Cooling the fire inside allowed for the ocean of emotion to come forth.

I could finally see free of the bias of my own negativity. This was evident in my behavioral changes specifically my change of speech and what I started speaking about. I was always ashamed to speak of certain things that made me look weak and vulnerable. I was afraid to speak about my true emotions, afraid to be judged and shamed. That changed and with it I stopped swearing and cursing so much, I didn't need to anymore. My heart rate started going down. Almost 30% in the end. I spoke softer. I didn't even realize until these things were brought to my attention. Then suddenly I didn't recognize myself. No one recognized me. I was still in that day dream that had become my life like a new born child experiencing things for the first time. A lot of the old triggers had disappeared. I was alone and for the first time I was okay to spend time with myself. I even learnt to dance and whilst I wasn't very good it didn't bother me because it made me really happy. With time I began to loosen up and dancing became a beautiful expression of unwinding from the fear of feeling embarrassed. I spent time chalk drawing my walls full of flowers and ribbons seeing the energy flowing through me and around me in waves of color and music. With all my practice I could use both hands at the same time like a conductor ordering my inner orchestra, writing a new song of life. I was seeing the geometrics in all its organized patterns, realizing that nature is balance and just like the flower I could be that order, beautifully simple and yet infinitely complex- if I continued searching for the equilibrium according to the sequences of the Codex Fingerprint.

Not too long ago I knew nothing of these things. Now I was understanding it. Seeing the connections in unity not separation. Seeing my reflection in its harmony through the geometry that is there for all to see and I was choosing to view with lit eyes opened once more. I began to understand how a collective consciousness could manifest things beyond our conception. I began to see the power and potential of unity and I was starting to speak the truth I knew.

Chapter 7

The power of self-exposure

I was a new born to this spoken word in a world where diplomacy and censorship dictates what truth is. I was learning to speak up when needed for the sake of that truth. Not that I was forced or no one else would but because I chose to. It became easier to not be drawn into previous cycles I was free from, simply recognizing these cycles in observation. This allowed me to concentrate my energy on more important matters. Thus I spent more time inward engaging with myself in a more uplifting way. Listening to the guidance from the all of the universe inside. Learning that every vibration has its purpose, even the ones whose colors I did not yet know. Love and its thorns amidst the roses. It may appear absent at times but this is a perceptive problem in a world of prejudice. In a world of love we know we are all equally separated only by the position of the growth of the soul, I understood this now. In unity wisdom rules the lands of the free not tyrants. In unity we all strive for the common good of all man not just a few. In unity we aspire to the union of the collective, not the separation individualistic needs. We have been separated through class, color, sex, denomination and many more yet we all bleed the same color blood with the same skeletons. The imbalance of this dualistic expression has caused the decay of ourselves and the society we have created. We see this in the way we treat ourselves, our homeless, our animals, our food, our lack of respect for nature, our ruthless cruelty toward innocent victims of wars that are illegal and unjustified yet no rectification is done by the very organizations setup to prevent this in the first place. I watch the Palestinian people being tortured by an Israel who themselves were victims of that same cruelty. Why would they want to inflict that suffering on another? Why does the very powers that have fought against foreign invasion and rule praise a country like that? Jew hates Muslims who hates Christian who hates Jews yet we all supposedly serve the same loving creator? Collectively we have broken the laws of humanity. We have become the unnatural way. What we don't realize is that the universe doesn't take sides and the law is clear with regards to this. What you take you must give or else the balance will not be restored for you.

We are guilty and though it may be hard to judge ourselves we must but we don't, instead we cause fear rather than admit we are afraid of judgement and exposure. Many persons today who causes fear are themselves the result of abusive pasts. They project their pain and weakness onto others claiming to be the resolution to the very problem they are the creators of. We see this at a macrocosm level with our Government who searches for binding resolutions to problems they've created with the policies that favor one over the other. They seek to right wrongs in other countries when their own countries are no better. They sell propaganda as truth and we the people simply accept it as such, never considering that someone may have an agenda that surpasses our understanding. Here the people are guilty. At a microcosm level we see this in people equally always trying to guide and advise others on their households and affairs when they themselves do not live by the very advice they give, it cannot be stated enough.

The very government voted into power does not provide the change they promise in their campaigning, strangely they are not held accountable? Even stranger is the people continue to vote these very organizations back into power. Why would anyone continue to vote for the same lies over and over? Do we not have the power to govern ourselves?

The government serves a purpose when they do their job. When they don't the people do not have the same power to remove them as they had to vote them into power in the first place. Why do we have to wait for elections several years later when the problem is right now? God forbid we try other means we are seen as anarchists or domestic terrorists. Egos rules the world masked as goodness. For the most part we don't care enough anymore to stand together to make the world a better place because in part we are the same, isolated by selfishness and self-interest. We sit on the fence pointing fingers hoping no one will point at us and when someone does we kick and scream as loud as possible to deflect from the cold truth of our apathy.

It is our fault when we see the expansion of our own consciousness manifest as those we put into power all be it the part we choose to ignore and pretend like it doesn't exist. We hate wars and yet we have tempers, we claim to care for nature and yet our greed and need for convenience destroys the very nature we claim to care for. I am no different. In some way you have met before many times. I am the feared, the doubtful, the frustration, the ego that masks the fear. In my weakness I created your habits you thought was just who you were. I am the perfect man you thought would make a good husband one day. I was a liar and I did many things that today I'm not proud of. I as bad as you can imagine and whilst these energies exist in us all not everyone is that way but not everyone is loved either and not everyone shares love.

I learnt to hug people in my life. To hug someone and give all of myself to them even if just for a moment. To share my energy with anyone and everyone. Nobody could take from me anymore because I chose to give. I had no expectation of receiving anything in return, not anymore. It wasn't always like that but it made me a better person and allowed me to set myself free from the monster I once was that at times I did not contain and mostly chose not to contain.

That day another dark shadow left me. This time I was better prepared. I could again see it standing outside watching and waiting. I stood looking at myself once more and said…"For me it is done, I no longer need you as part of me." I was more than the shadow and it was time to let go. *"This is the power of the growing light within when goodness is the provocateur of the next step in your life dear reader."* I found myself humbled and not entitled and began to embrace this better way. I was finding the beauty in the broken and the power of appreciation. *"There is only one truth and that is love and applying the loving truth creates the divine purpose as we begin to live in music. As long as we live in that divine purpose our light will never leave us because we will never leave ourselves. The gift of life and these words were hiding in the spaces between here and there."*

It takes patience to nurture the light growing inside. It takes time to see a thing that you did not know existed. When you become the creator you will find it is harder to create when you know the law you do not yet know is inside. That's what free will does in all its infinite confusion.

"Hold he in balance the seven and thy body will retain the strength of the whole. I if thy be old thy body will freshen and thy strength will become as a youth" Emerald *tablets*. In these spaces of silent mind I was able to reverse time. Not time as we know it. Changing things from our earlier life that affects our present life. Freeing others from the grip of our bondage changes their lives and health too. This may sound strange however consider the power these words? I applied this which today I know is the highest truth and through introspection I was able to begin to see the truth of my parent's relationships when I looked at my own failed relationships observing the similarities. I was no longer blinded by the emotions of old. Through the rectification that forgiveness brings and with clear eyes the truth was right in front of me. Through the years I chose to overlook many things. Some things I didn't want to see when I grew older. I used my sisters to see into my mother's past as we all share the same blood, history and circumstance. I looked at the domineering nature of their personalities and behavior and could see my mother as I began to remember what I had chosen to forget. I could finally see what I was not ready to see before but I could not force another to see as I did. I learnt this through my many failures. I looked at my own affairs and mistakes, traced my own self-righteous attitude and failings. I observed my own anger and began to create an alignment of symmetry between everything as I had done with every other aspect of this journey to find clarity in the distortion of this most difficult aspects of mind. I tried to understand father's thought patterns and why he did what he did? What was happening in his mind space? Even today some of the choices he makes

doesn't make a lot of sense to me and yet it makes perfect sense to him. What were the reasons because anyone can be analyzed today who is still cycling in yesterday and one can gain a deeper understanding when the emotions that blinds us are removed in favor of the truth impossible to see when we are to close. Without bias I could look deeper. I asked what was going through my head because some of the things I did was no better. I was able to let go the most savage events that led defining moments of my young life with a new perspective and grew from it. I stopped trying to hide it, stopped overlooking it. Making peace with my likeness to my own father allowed me to be one with the unlearnt history. Thus I could find the answers when I began to answer myself with absolute honestly. I began to trust myself as the fear subsided through the time spent in the dark sometimes misguidedly pushing the limits beyond the law. These limits are a part of the construct I didn't fully understand back then.

One evening earlier on searching deep within the angles I crossed barriers I knew I wasn't supposed to. It was a few days in and I was so far inside. I couldn't tell the difference between this world and where I was. I should have stepped back, taken time to assess because nothing seemed right, everything was distorted and unreal. The wind blew my gates open as I stood between the angles. I knew what I had done and I knew the consequences but I never experienced those consequences as I've only ever read of them in the ancient texts. I regretted what I did and didn't know how to undo it or if it even could be undone. I begged forgiveness, tried to fight my way out of that space with those things that was all around me. It felt like everywhere I looked there was something coming toward me. I tried everything I could, turning to the mechanisms used in spiritual practices. Nothing worked. It felt like the whole world was being pulled into me wherever I looked. I ran down to the ocean intending to drown myself as I thought what I was doing would destroy the world. I closed my eyes lying on the grass begging forgiveness over and over for what I know I had done. I saw things that night that affected me deeply. I saw fears and a darkness which I didn't know was inside all at once as the hounds caught up to me in the spaces I should not have been at the edges of times end.

Taking responsibility was the only reason I made it through. I was wrong, I knew what I had done, in the end I couldn't negotiate with the law even though I tried. That evening something was born inside of me into this world. My vision changed permanently. As time has passed I've learnt to respect the law more and no longer use the angles to the extent as I did before. Now I choose to earn my way as a student of this great universe immersing myself in the experience of the growth that comes from life's lessons. I learnt the power of moderation that evening and whilst in honesty I have tested the boundaries many times over I have done so knowing the consequences because we can never know a thing if it's just out of our reach but the right way is to earn the way. I will say that these spaces are sacred and they must be respected or we risk the cataclysmic results the ancients suffered.

The strange angles

In the Tablets it reads..."*Time moves through strange angles, yet only through curves could I hope to find the key to the time space...*" These angles that I discovered allowed me to penetrate the spaces between here and there when I was completely out of alignment. They are ever present yet lay just out of our knowing. It is like the error of parallax. At least this is the easiest way for me to describe it.

(A parallax error is the perceived shift in an object's position as it is viewed from different angles. Parallax error is an error caused by humans, while measuring a quantity if your eye is not at the proper angle to the scale you're reading, it will cause parallax error. It only depends upon the line of sight.)

I call it the gap where infinity lives and if you use the geometry in the book you will find the angle that creates the movement. This gap allows you to see things beyond the limitations of comprehensive understanding. This alone will not show you the map. The right way is through the releasing and freeing of the self, this creates automatic alignment. To achieve that requires the position of mind and self within time and space to which love and truthful intent are the only keys that will unlock the door. In the Tablets it reads… *"Found I only by moving upward, and then rightward could I be free of the time of the movement"*

This has multiple meanings. Consider the whole earth was a grid. 1 cubit by 1 cubit separated by different quadrants of existence. In the beginning I would physically move 4 paces up and 1 pace to the right using my house tiles which were 520mm x 520mm. *"Other chambers I built and left vacant to all seeming, yet within them are the keys to amenti"*…*Emerald Tablets* I used the angles of the pyramid shafts projecting my eyes into the sky, water, earth, stars etc. and observed any changes in mind or in actual space interpreting the texts differently because I knew that when one overlays the pyramid with the human head the angles represented something, likewise when one overlays the pyramid with the human torso. Slowly changes were noted. This took years to achieve the results as the resistance fell to the flow off the right way. I learnt the not blinking access key by accident when I would forget to blink as I was staring into space. I learnt to bind frequencies and this allowed for a higher communication both inward and outward. As time went on with the expansion of inner growth created the geometric visualization that began to manifest. This is especially noticeable in the night sky and must be experienced to be understood. Then you will know that the sky is more than you think in its geometric order.

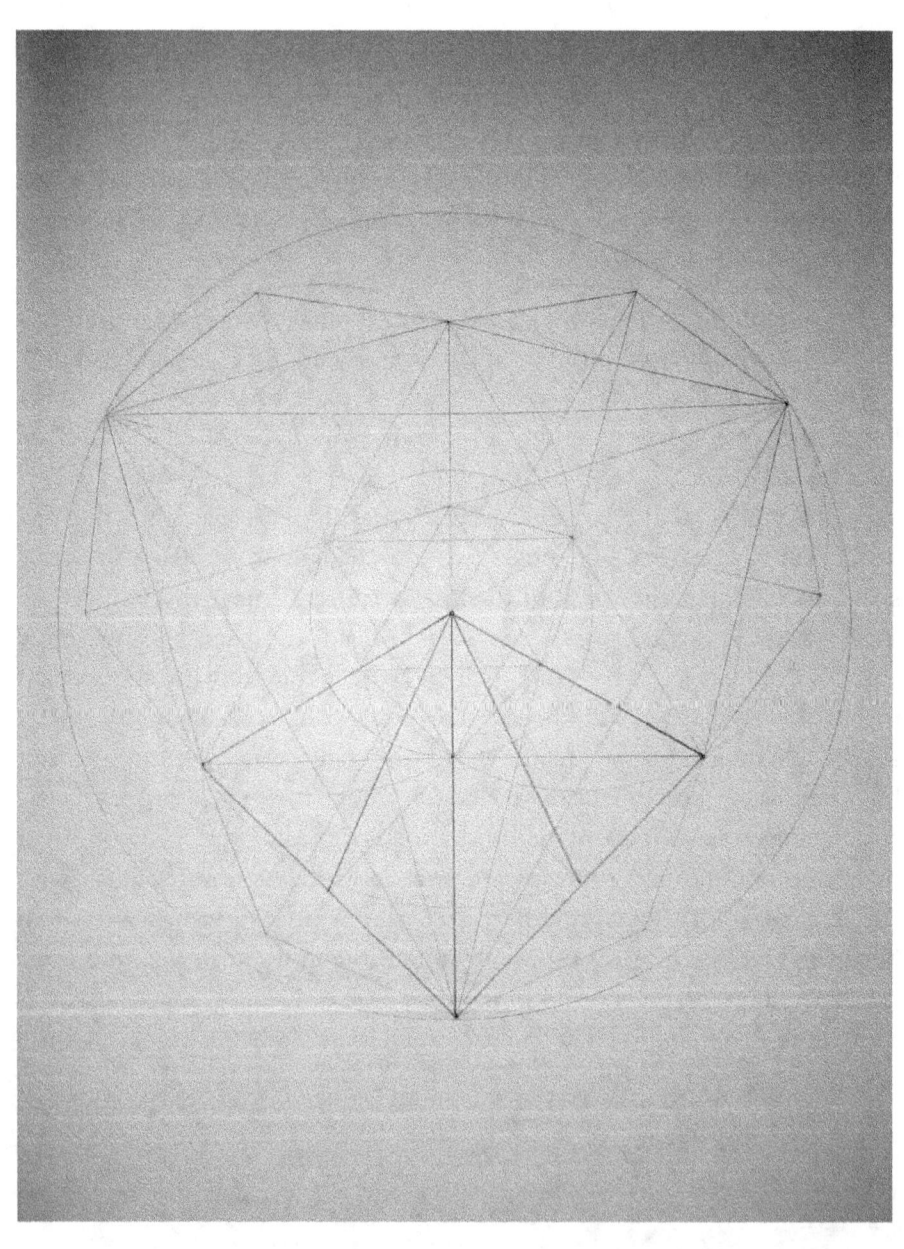

Interlocking the inner and outer self allows us to see further into the forgotten the truth lost for all the ages thus bridging the gap between the self and the divine self. The eight sides is actually designed to show us the optical illusion that exist between the space of this world and the next. This can be seen when straight lines created in the strange angles bends, see first image.

Chapter 8

The Great Pyramid

I began to make sense of the ancient mysteries in ways I had never thought possible. I could see with a unified eye what the ancients tried to show us through the first time and their original monuments. Understanding there purpose and realizing their intention. We are a fractal version of the great pyramid, a torus of expanding and contracting energy that breathes as we do, hence the tunnels and water needed to make the connection. We are as the moon is to earth and just like the moon radiates its own light from within so too the pyramid was built from the inside out. Just like the human heart is the first organ to form then is enclosed by the rest of the growing body. Its design and purpose was a collective of several applications, healing, ascending, initiation, energy generator, frequency amplifier and stabilizer. Multiple layers just like the human. It's meant to be dark inside for in this dark space lay the light hidden within.

We are the capstone, it lies between our eyes deep inside. One in the one in balance upon the right vibration, the light born will see the perfect geometry amidst the green haze of the emerald hue, holographic in its representation. It is within us all and doesn't require imagination, it requires flow (etheric flow). When we begin to unwind ourselves we begin to unlock the pathways inside and activate the code past the resistive nature of the lower vibrational self through the mirror higher expression.

The earth like the sky is a map. The complexes built by the ancients were designed amongst other things to guide us back to the wisdom lost since the times of the dwellers. To hold our consciousness and wonder about the unanswerable questions. On Easter Island the statues are in the volcano was placed there with purpose. The statues show metaphysically the gateway to UNAL and how to access the inner most self through the false door. Today we say it is impossible to do what they did and yet we have never tried, imagine a whole civilization working toward a singular purpose. Today we chase our own goals. This was the difference between us and them, just like particle arrangement in magnetic objects vs nonmagnetic objects. We are not the same yet we are equally no different.

The geometry of truth

"Forth from equilibrium came the great cycles, moving in harmony toward infinities end. Know ye O man that far in the space time, Infinity too shall pass into change, hear ye and list to the voice of Wisdom, Know that all is part of all evermore." Emerald Tablets I was shown this and many things. I was shown how the universe works with its cycles transferring one age to a next. There are cycles within cycles that fractals into infinity and yet is predictable by its nature. A collective awareness of this will bring changes to the infinite image of the reality we know and I began to understand this. If the collective mind is separated then depending on the collective resonance may have no effect and thus the default will continue to play out in separation. Organizations aware of this easily use the mechanisms like the media to shape global consciousness, creating and influencing global events that on the surface appears random. Know that nothing is random and our limitless power is governed only by the differential of knowing and the absence of awareness of that knowing. At the right vibration we can do the unthinkable.`

Consider a time in human history called the Younger Dryas event, still disputed by modern science. The Younger Dryas is one of the most well-known examples of abrupt change. About 14,500 years ago. Earth's climate began to shift from a cold glacial world to a warmer interglacial state and through this transition, temperatures in the Northern Hemisphere suddenly returned to near-glacial conditions. This near-glacial period is called the Younger Dryas, named after a flower Dryas octopetala that grows in cold conditions and that became common in Europe during this time. The end of the Younger Dryas about 11,500 years ago was particularly abrupt. In Greenland temperatures rose 10°C

(18°F) in a decade (Alley 2000). Other proxy records, including varved lake sediments in Europe, also display these abrupt shifts (Brauer et al. 2008).

The Younger Dryas is clearly observable in paleoclimate records from many parts of the world. In the Cariaco Basin north of Venezuela for example, temperatures decreased about 3°C (5.5°F) although some of this cooling might have been due to greater upwelling of colder subsurface water (Lea et al. 2003). In many parts of the Northern Hemisphere tropics conditions also became drier (Hughen et al. 2000; Wang et al. 2001).

The Younger Dryas occurred during the transition from the last glacial period into the present interglacial (the Holocene). During this time, the North American or Laurentide ice sheet was rapidly melting and adding freshwater to the ocean. Scientists have hypothesized that, just prior to the Younger Dryas, meltwater fluxes were rerouted from the Mississippi River to the St. Lawrence River. Geochemical evidence from ocean sediment cores supports this idea (Carlson et al. 2007), although other possible routings such as to the Mackenzie River cannot be ruled out presently. A more northerly routing of meltwater has a greater impact on the salinity and density of the surface ocean in the North Atlantic which can cause a slowing of the ocean's thermohaline circulation and climate changes around the world. Multiple proxies for the thermohaline circulation indicate that such changes occurred during the Younger Dryas (McManus et al. 2004; Praetorius et al. 2008; Lynch-Stieglitz et al. 2011). Eventually, as the meltwater flux abated, the thermohaline circulation strengthened again and climate recovered.

The record from Dome C in Antarctica supports this explanation. If the thermohaline circulation were to slow, less heat would be transported from the South Atlantic to the North Atlantic. This would cause the South Atlantic to warm and the North Atlantic to cool. This pattern, sometimes called the "bipolar see-saw," is observable when comparing the GISP2 and Dome C records for the Younger Dryas (EPICA Community Members 2004).

During this timeline it has also been theorized that comet strikes occurred, further theories have suggested that approximately 12,000 years ago there was a displacement of the Earth's crust. The entire outer shell of the earth moved approximately 2,000 miles. When the Earth's crust shifted all of Antarctica was encapsulated by the polar zone. At the same time North American was released from the Arctic Circle and became temperate. This is based on the theory of Continental Drift - Earth's continents slowly drifting apart over millions of years. This is possible because the outer crust of the Earth floats upon a semi-liquid layer.

A pole shift theory is a hypothesis based on geologic evidence that the physical north and south poles of Earth have not always been at their present-day locations; in other words, the axis of rotation had shifted. Pole shift theory is almost always discussed in the context of Earth, but other solar system bodies may have experienced axial reorientation during their existences. In Maps of the Ancient Sea Kings he supported the suggestion made by Arlington Mallery that a part of the Piri Reis Map was a depiction of the area of Antarctica known as Queen Maud Land. He used this map to propose that a 15° pole shift occurred around 9,600 BCE (approx. 11,600 years ago) and that a part of the Antarctic was ice-free at that time, and that an ice-age civilization could have mapped the coast. He concludes that "Antarctica was mapped when these parts were free of ice", taking that view that an Antarctic warm period coincided with the last ice age in the Northern hemisphere, and that the Piri Reis and other maps were based on "ancient" maps derived from ice-age originals.

Viewing these events from a collective consciousness influence it makes better sense and is easier to comprehend when you add the collective cycle of energy of humanity with the greater cycles of the cosmos and its alignment. Consider the self and its resistance vs flow and the temperature changes that results. This can be observed in electrical circuits where the amount of resistance is directly proportional to heat. Whilst we have no knowledge anymore of the greater laws these alignments can also cause disasters like comets or earthquakes if we collectively cross through barriers we're not supposed to, breaking the cosmic law as a collective consciousness, or raising and/or lowering our collective vibration. This is how the physical manifested fractal we works. This is in the higher chakras and equally the lower chakras. This in alignment with greater cyclic movements creates the physical effect of the metaphysical cause. That is why it is so important to treat this journey and yourself with loving goodness and have your heart lead the way or together in the laws of absence we bring about the end of what we know as it has done many times before. Then the master reset starts it all over again as it has through the infinite cycles of earth's existence. One epoch ending and another beginning, collectively and also individually. One human can raise his or her consciousness to a level where you may affect the whole.

For anyone who doubts the law of one consider the world is much older than we know. Ancient man has at times in pre-history existed at a vibration of unity, not duality but was equally man. Harmoniously living in balance with nature and self. Verify for yourself. Answer the questions about the Megalithic sites older than 10000 years before all religions existed. Today we cannot account for this so it is simply ignored but that doesn't make it any less true. The dualistic nature of self and our ignorance doesn't allow for this comprehension. We bind our self to this ignorance but usually start with good intentions and lose our self in the distorted justification of misperception from what we claim is to what actually is. Our mind influences those around us as they in turn influence us because they are us as we are them.

I now knew that I had never lived from the true heart even though I thought I did. I was always far out of true alignment. It's still challenging keeping it open and being born of fire didn't help with patience and tolerance. It was easier for me to burn things down than to build things up in the spirit of the old way. I could see how I could and did become trapped here, lost to my own suffering created by my own choices. I too was learning to live in the love the heart brings.

I will say that re-orientation is not easy in a world of convenience where it's easier to buy food than to cook it. Very few grows their own food anymore. Most of life has become automated and we have become lazy and isolated to the extent where most people don't even know their neighbors. Admitting this is hard but here we must or we will fail until we give up. If we have the will then we will fail our way to the lesson we will learn in the end when we persevere. I chose to apply the 42 virtues of MA'AT. If you judge the Egyptians then honor your own codex. What direction does your inner compass point to? The same humanity that lives separate can equally create harmony. This is the building blocks of unity. Duality is the divide and conquer that comes with what labels bring. Putting up one against the other, Christian and Muslim, brother and sister, father and mother. When I removed myself from the labels I unbound myself from my separation and humanity.

Unfortunately we tend toward the creation of separation so easily. We fight for feminism and capitalism, communism and every other ism that is, for what? We claim that some lives matter when all lives matter. We keep tearing each other apart robbing each other and mother earth killing the flame within till in the end every living soul hates the image they see in the mirror. We don't have to die we simply suffer every day passing onto the next generation the same fear that created the cycle in the beginning. Consider the value of this mindset, its origins and its conclusions. Consider our current course, consider your course in your life thus far. Consider the battles you fight and the victories you take. Consider who you destroy and how you make the next human being feel in your pursuit of happiness. Consider how we define happiness. We can never be happy when its' built on these kinds of victories. True victory comes from using your will to give without expectation. This is the simplest formula for absolute success.

The flower of life taught me to see myself as all. It was not easy and still isn't but it is worth the effort. Taking the time to learn of love's great power and the many other beautiful things that I had forgotten. We do not need to wait until we are destroyed before we find the true meaning of purpose. Every day is a new opportunity to grow from the same day. That's what I've learnt being a little more patient and kind seems like foreign words to some and yet to others is a way of life. This was the love I was working my way back to.

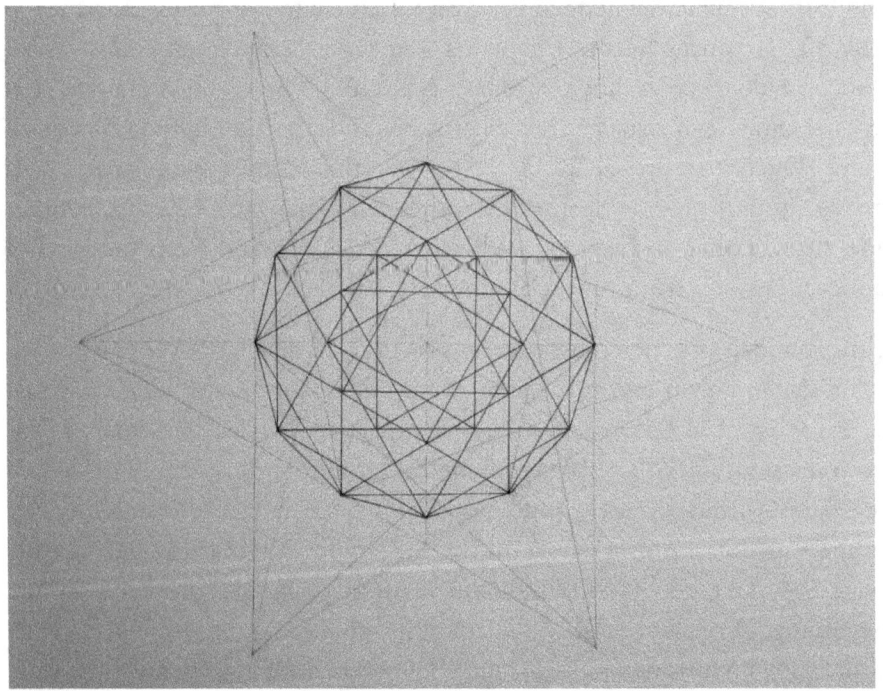

The sacred key of geometry

It was in the pursuit of this love that I found the sacred keys within the geometry. It upgraded and rewired my mind. Understanding when and how to use them is the key that would take a while to know until in the end it wasn't needed anymore. The ability to draw the geometry from mind alone means the circuits inside are wired. Don't try to memorize the geometry as this will bring failure instead see your thoughts change as you draw, observe the accuracy with which you draw. I made the drawings an extension of myself as with everything else. I saw how the details expanded as I expanded and equally contracted when I did. The angles and curves would reflect my position of mind. The more complex the drawing the more still the mind is. The ability to create fractal expansions both inward and outward opened my mind space to a higher level of comprehension. I suggest you save your first drawing for reference later, compare and see the transformation of self with the perfection of the geometry… *"Find the truth in your life and you will find the way. Hold your vibration there. The rest will fall into place according to your purpose"* Raising my awareness changed my perception which changed my comprehension and that in turn it was changing my reality. Some things must be experienced and yet on some level we already know these things. The Tablets like all ancient texts cannot show everything and at times they are veiled in such heavy codex that without the experience and right vibration it would be impossible to decipher. Application is the key, just like drawing the geometry is a key, at first unknown then known.

Do not chase the ether in the main stream, you will not find it there. I didn't find it there. I wasted a lot of time searching for answers in the wrong direction following paths that many times ended nowhere. It is what it is, I learnt as I grew. In time as I learnt to trust myself more I stop looking outward anyway. I began to remember that the truth I sort lies only within. Only a cool fire opened the door that allowed me to come down to earth and find my zero point. This is where the battle must be fought first, knowing the right and left, up and down, inside and out and then balancing it in purpose which is another difficult journey all on its own. These keys at times may appear more than you may think and beyond our reach but it has to be cryptic because actually it is simpler than you think. Many times I've been overwhelmed and at times angry with the simplicity of infamy. Here is one key – THOTH is TRUTH. The highest truth creates immediate alignment with the infinite wave. You can find the wave with truth's absence but you'll not be able to hold the vibration. As such it is protected from the liars and the unwilling. They who have unlocked it will know the order of it. Thus with the truth inside and the knowing it brings one can always call out anyone to describe this order and should you not be able to describe it we will know, we always know.

I began to note the overlapping energy fields plotting it according to cyclic time allowing me to feel the energy flowing up and down, in and out rhythmically stable when it was stable. Working with cyclic time removes the distraction of the systems linear based time and thinking through self-observation, exploring and understanding the evolving self. Start within a cycle and begin to track your thoughts and moods. Also use the daily cycle with the sunrise and sunset being your reference to cyclic revolutions, the same can be applied to lunar cycles. Check your thoughts first thing in the morning and compare them at 6pm in the evening. Sleeping is a rectifier hence it becomes the best reference for the actual self likewise at 6pm the shadow self is in full effect. The differential of self will determine the gap in alignment. The consistency with which you are able to blend from one wavelength to another allows you to plot using the chakras how and where you are within the fractal cycle and the condition of that energy within the cycle. When you have mastered the cycles this will no longer apply. Till then check for moods and thoughts and how they change, these are energies that are out of alignment and may be blocked. Remember energy is always flowing however, if you are not aware for you it doesn't exist and you cannot partake in the life giving light it offers. This is important to note and I struggled to comprehend this. There is only one day, the greater cycles are only relevant in the unification of self and humanity.

The world has cycled through its beginning and its beginnings end many times over. The greater cycles requires continuous observation to plot a cyclic age thus predicting the collective energy change. If you do not fear death which you shouldn't then this should never concern you. You are the creator of life and death hence fear can never be a factor in this unified expression. Thus unity and harmony exists without fear. Everything is always in divine order based on the law. It is when we break the law that the consequences are manifest in totality. We see evidence today of this in ancient times whilst beyond some of our current comprehension consider that there were others here greater than us, long before us yet equal as us. Just observe the evidence of the cataclysms that have come and gone as I have spoken of before. Its's available for all to see. The establishment is lying, you don't need to have special skills to verify this. Time will tell if we can change the path earth is on or not. Either way the default seemingly random nature of the cosmos is governed by the law so if we create disasters within us it will manifest. If we create hope it will manifest equally. Thus what do you give your deepest unconscious and conscious thoughts to?

When I came to understand this I realized that truth sometimes comes from an argument. Not the arguing that we are familiar with. This was a vibratory expression with truth as the center. Sometimes it is needed to lower and at times heighten one's vibration to bridge the gap and communicate the required message. This way arguing is simply constructive debating when the heart leads the way in unlocking the self and another from a vibration they are trapped in or limited by. There is no "agree to disagree." It took a few hard lessons to know this and I was kicked out of a couple of houses for standing up for that truth. This is also how I learnt about how powerful others' triggers are. It also taught me the nature of unified separation of shared reality. Gaining consciousness of this network is a developmental process that has been taking place over the generations. Scientists, philosophers and other researchers have long considered nature as a single whole, we are part of that whole. The very idea that we emerged from a zero single point, cycling through time's linear perception. When we examine nature, we see these cycles and the law in operation, we see the tides come and go, we see life born to seed new life after. If we fail to see these laws completely, either on macro or micro scales, it merely reflects our incomplete knowledge and perception. The more we discover about nature, the more we discover its absolute interconnectedness and interdependence. When we know that we are nature we can finally bridge the gap. I could understand this now in a way that was different from before, this time with a deep sense of empathy. Whilst one cannot force another to see what they are not ready to see one has to find the courage to stand up for what is right and live by the example of that right despite knowing the potential consequences and this brought me a renewed sense of peace and purpose, in the spirit of the natural way.

Intimidation, debating and the fear it instilled no longer served me. Thus I further refined my speech from the inside using compassion instead of condemnation. Including empathy without enablement as a means to bridge the gap without instilling fear, retraction and repression. This brought very positive results and quelled the need for aggressive confrontations because I was speaking from the heart in truth and love.

When I started drawing the more complex geometry I ask if in infamy there wasn't a simpler way of constructing complex shapes without modern geometric law. I believed that there were

proportions that could be found that would allow for these creations. This image is created only using those proportions which originates from the inner most circle and likewise the inner most self.

One must be able to enter the spaces before the trigger so as to affect positive and lasting change without being demonized when one's intention is not to hurt another. How does one bypass the automated trigger? In the beginning I couldn't answer this. It was because of a problem I knew existed inside of me. My fear of rage, I knew this from my earliest childhood witnessing the effects of rage. I always kept clear of the chaos of rage. I was afraid of becoming what I once hated and doing the very thing I swore I'd never do even though I found myself guilty of doing many other things along the way.

This would prove to be very difficult. I had no experience with rage. I simply never went into those spaces my whole life so for me it was a black void of nothingness. Ironically that's what chaos is but I knew there was more there to be found. With the risks associated I embarked on releasing myself from other defective states of mind that could be worked on more easily. Being afraid of rage and the chaos it brings had to be dealt with at some stage even if not immediately. I knew there were other aspects of myself I could work on so I did just that. I had theorized that the more I could release the easier it would be to step into the dark chaos of rage. I found myself spending even more time at the ocean enjoying the water's cooling effect. I increased my step count per day and was achieving it. I had converted my detox and affirmations into a semi standard way of living. I had given away half the things in my house and decided that the house itself was blocking my progress, with a degree of apprehension but with faith in this journey I decided to sell it. This was a very big step. In the months before the house was sold I brought more plants inside, started using pine oils, sage, lavender, pine needles, frankincense and murr which I burnt to partake in the vibrations it brings and because it smelt really nice. I began smoking less, drinking less and took up a friend's offer to travel for a while. I ended my career and took time to see the world with these new eyes.

As the self begins to expand so too does the geometry, changing in form, changing in meaning as the the self grows into a new dimension of being

I learnt to stop overthinking and start flowing even more which was still challenging because I had given up the security of my income and residence. Despite the concern the lessons it brought could not have been learnt otherwise but I was still occupied with mixed emotions toward the teachers in this world. The simplicity of some of the mightiest wisdoms which have been overlooked presented a degree of frustration. It becomes a challenge of fortitude to persevere through the abyss of the dark night of the soul to find something that only exists in the darkness of the unknown. I wanted time to experience the light of this journey here. I decided to stop drinking and smoking for a 90day detox aligned with the law. This was easier than expected yet whilst the thought of drinking faded quickly, smoking kept creeping up and with it I noticed myself suppressing my speech and that was followed with the need to eat. Thus I changed my diet to only include superfoods mostly eaten raw, this created a balance whilst not ideal at least allowed for movement in the right direction.

It was during this time that new knowledge revealed itself as I began to release myself from the potholes of my low vibration. I lost many friends on this journey as I began to see what I could not previously see. There were special people in my life I had grown very close to and they had helped me so extensively in unlocking many aspects of the true self. Losing them were one of the highest prices that had to be paid for what was to be would come from the experience of the pain it caused.

I asked them of the resentment they held inside. I knew them well and knew of their histories. I asked them of the past and the anger that became clearer to see the less angry I became. I asked them on the basis of what we had experienced together and what they claimed their objectives were to release what was inside. I had realized that there was resentment inside me still so I chose to release it. Every time they would pause and sadly decided not to release. In the beginning I couldn't understand. Their desire for retribution was more powerful than the will to forgive. Despite all they had witnessed and all they had claimed, sadly it wasn't enough. This is the power of what we hold inside. We can never blame anything except ourselves and whilst there are dark energies that exist we give rise to them and then allow them in with what we give our thoughts too because it opens the gateways. I knew this now. There is no magic here and it's automated and I have seen its operations. When we separate ourselves from our histories we separate ourselves from what we create. Here our beliefs are not relevant as this is part of a cycle that extends past man's understanding.

Some things I didn't want to see even after I released I ignored the signs just like I did in the past. I tried as much as I could to help and share the value of this side of letting go instead of holding onto that negative. I never thought that their pain would be stronger than the relationship we shared, I never even considered it. I never knew about the limitations because I never knew who they really were. I never knew they were never planning on releasing that thing and was never going to tell me about it, why did they lie? Why wasn't I worth the truth? It devastated me every time making the hardest choice to continue moving onward when they wouldn't. I still think about the growth that came from making those decisions vs the pain of the lesson because I would've done anything for every one of them. I didn't want to have to learn these lessons that way. Many of my life's plans was forced to change many times. They were the red dragon, the many heads of the one whole. I saw my mommy all over again. All I wanted to do was help and at times when the help was rejected I was consumed by confusion that brought hatred which I suppressed. I didn't want to argue, I didn't want to trust what I knew and felt. Instead I would go back to the drawing board trying to figure out another way because…"Maybe I missed something?" I never considered that I was looking at it from the wrong perspective or to even look at it from another perspective. Many times I would blame and punish myself for missing something. What I am speaking of may not be present in every single person, sometimes pain may be inherited or else you wouldn't have chosen to be here to begin with. The end can only be seen at the end until you know the beginning. Thus all the striving created the ability to communicate today the things that was impossible yesterday and be able to prove and replicate the things I didn't understand a year ago but Saying goodbye each time was so hard and never got easier. The pain tested my self-worth causing an emptiness in a heart once filled with love. I was shattered and each time it hurt like the first time.

Long ago I remember my mommy walking down the street and I chasing after her. She told me to go away, chasing me away as I got closer. I shouted in tears…"MOMMY please don't chase me away, whatever you need just tell me and we can do it. I'll take you anywhere you want to go just stop, please I'm begging you." She used to call me her "right hand" she knew I would do anything for her yet all she could say was…"You can't take me where I want to go." I felt so small. I knew what it meant, I was older and not as blinded by the warrior self that would die for her without question. No less it made me feel like a dog not a son. I wasn't a dog and I didn't deserve to get chased away that way. All I wanted to do was help and it broke my heart to know that I couldn't do anything. It took something from me that I didn't know how to put it back. Those were the moments where I had lost the fight inside of me. It took many years but I finally grew stronger when I understood who everyone was but even this is difficult to ease the suffering one feels when rejected so badly. It made me think that such a small percentage of self has such absolute power. It served as a dark reminder of the impossible nature of this journey. It is this small percentage that will make us have to re-walk it all again because everything we created in goodness masks the rotten root and the doubt of not knowing who we truly are will never subside. It will always occupy a space we will never penetrate or know to penetrate. It will have to be up-rooted to allow a new yet same tree to grow. This tree is the spirit of life. We can never know this till we remove it all but having to start all over is something most will never do and so we must repeat this life until we do one after the other with no memory as guidance only the whispers that makes us wonder whether we had been here before. I said to my mommy quietly as she took her last breaths…"The secrets I know I'll take to the grave, no one can hurt you anymore, you free now" and in doing so I bound myself for many years, lost in those secrets that distorted my mind.

Good people suffer never realizing they are being manipulated and misled. We have a duty to stop this. Sadly those most guilty of this don't even recognize that they are doing anything wrong. It's hard making peace when I too was guilty of the same thing for so long. I am no angel but then I never pretended to be. Pleading ignorance here was not good enough, not anymore and my heart was sore again. The people in our life may not be as they seem to be but the pain is still real. It felt like a cruel joke the universe had played on me and I had to fight so hard not to shut down but I didn't because I stopped shutting down. My self-worth had evolved because I had found my compass and I knew what I deserved. I was worth more than a lie and I found the courage not to give in ever again.

My mommy suffered and there was nothing I could do because there is nothing you can do when someone chooses bondage. The pain was more powerful than the freedom that forgiveness could've brought. I watched cancer kill her heart then her mind long before it killed her body. For most of my life I found myself blaming my father for our families' history. He was guilty of many things but so was my mother, so was I. None of us were innocent. Everyone claimed to be right, no one considered that they may be wrong. It's one of the reasons I've struggled to say I'm sorry for so long. It's a lesson that took me years to even consider and came at the cost of good relationships forged in the fires of the unlearnt.

Despite it all when I do engage now I use my heart and speak only the truth whatever the cost. I have found that the effects today are far different than before. Truth and the heart it comes from speaks into creation a vibration that pierces all defenses. I am aware that our mouths have a deeper purpose and in truth we can find that purpose.

I found a part of me through this hell and kept moving onward. Understanding the purpose of my being more clearly than I ever had before. Healing takes patience with oneself and the courage to grow through the experience of the expression of the other side of love's beauty and not dissolving into the fire because of it. Healing is being present with the pain which is hard when the heart is raw and it's almost impossible to see any good. I thought I didn't care about anything, that wasn't true. The truth is I do care and I did care. I always cared that's why my heart broke so many times. People who care risk getting hurt. It's a strange way the universe works here and if you are not careful you can become very angry when you learn this. It isn't easy, however I was able to see the lessons both my parents tried to teach through the years, releasing myself from the anger and seeing the words for what they were. At its core the lessons had value even when they didn't live by everything they taught and made excuses for the things they knew they were guilty of. I could see them being trapped in their own cycles, a product of their free will and now my heart broke for them too. I had my freedom but those left were still bound and I could not affect any change other than provide an open heart for support and growth when it was required.

I was no longer bound by expending emotional energy thinking I could effect change that was not always possible. I no longer felt obligated to free anyone because everyone had a choice. I had broken the cycle. This would prove to be liberating and equally confusing. If all the world was meant to teach me something that means eventually, provided I learn and grow through the experience at some point I'll be alone all together as the trials of the outer would be complete, but I had been looking at it wrong all along. The lesson presented allows for a two way fractal to be created, learning, switching and growing or resetting and repeating, resetting means facing the same unknown except it's not really unknown. It is simply packaged differently, another circumstance but the same lesson repeating and it must be this way. These are the rules of the game of life. This lesson made so much sense. I could almost immediately see the purpose of the pain and the repeating cycles over and again as though for the first time with absolute understanding, it has always been the same pain.

For the very first time I found strength in the heartbreak and a renewed purpose as if I could change the direction of the wind at will. I had a look at the old once more with a better understanding of the limitations of infinity, this may sound strange thinking that infinity has limitations, it takes a moment to rationalize. Knowing these limitations and its operations allows one to grow past the limitations of the human condition and become something greater. Thus one can use the outer world to resolute the inner world when one knows the operational mechanisms of the outer world. It's all upside down because again it's designed that way just like the sphynx and its orientation where its rear end is actually the head of a human, this is one of its silent messages to us. These lessons can only be learnt through the experience of the finite and if we don't we wind ourselves up with what we resist creating the cycles of repeatability and this is what I never understood properly. I spent so much time searching for what I didn't understand in places, I didn't know because of my limited awareness of orientation when I already had all the tools- I needed to find my way. Silence exists in the storm when you remember what silence and the storm is equally.

This knowing is a gift of great power and gave me a deeper peace that was absent before. I now understood that when I was alone in the end everything would be resolved within. No more lessons to be presented but then I realized…"What if I was alone on earth and still had a list of unlearnt?" Whilst unlikely it is possible that I could be the last or only human on earth so I wouldn't know for sure. Thus I began to observe everything I did including where I looked at, what colors I saw, how my body reacted to certain things, using the bathroom, waking up at certain times, when I knocked my finger or toes. The synchronicities took on a new meaning because it is all relevant, absolutely everything. Now I knew that the mystic forest was not a forest in the same way comfort is not freedom, freedom is freedom. We can only know this when we walk the way. Freedom lies in the most obtuse places and I would go to the end of nowhere to find it. It is the 3% that governs our lives. That keeps us from the twelve and the one.

If your beauty appears to all you encounter as pure yet inside you carry a weight that doesn't show, regardless of the weight and regardless of your goodness the dark shadows that dwell in the 3% are blacker than anything you can mask and for those that chooses to see will see. Only you can tell the difference and knowing yourself makes that difference. If you feel even minutely uncomfortable ask the question why and have the courage to answer yourself. Something inside is offering you a clue. When you get closer to your freedom it may be close to impossible to spot this. We don't always want to hear or see the answers but sometimes we can easily overlook the obvious because it is veiled in the mirror image of goodness that isn't absolute. Absolution is either OR, before we can live in the middle point of zero we must first know the black and the white or else we are forever lost in the grey. This is the great test of the Universe. The hidden path of the children of light.

Chapter 9

What's your next step?

This pursuit of absolution does not have to take you to the seclusion of a far off place on a hill somewhere however if that calls to you then do it. Remember you are the nucleus and all is flowing around you, see it in the flower. The Knowing you seek may lie just outside in the dirt of the mud your feet no longer touch. If you think that the light is all that holds the keys you'll never make your way to the beyond. Like the IBIS Thoth found the Truth in the dirt buried where he could not see for it is only in the dark where the light ever glows. It is the sacrifice most will never consider that holds the keys of life. This is what defines one star from another in pursuit of the infinite wave. It is all that separates us. Our duty is to share the wisdom so that others too may grow and partake in the infinite all. In the modern world there are those that do not give willingly. Most are too afraid to lose the power the knowledge has brought so they sell it rather than share it. Selfishness is the disease that is slowly killing us in the separation it brings.

We have to deal with this frequency differential. For one, a thing means something completely different to another yet both is equally the same? We do not speak the same language anymore and have not done so for many generations. *"Once I tried to explain to someone once about the flashes of light and strange movements in the sky I witnessed this person could not perceive the explanation and later realized it was because I could not perceive the experience myself, I realized that the same words are used to communicate at all frequencies yet they do not mean the same and they are not interpreted the same and thus the meaning is lost without the awareness of the frequency differential."*

In the beginning I thought the experience was limited to me alone and I was too afraid to show others what I was experiencing. One by one more began to see what I saw and I began to understand how it worked even though I struggled to communicate it properly, it is a process that must be learnt from the beginning, there is no other way. The Truth and the way we express it is the key that unlocks physical transmutation as long as you can hold that vibration. It is the same for the ocean in the sky, the right vibration changes the starry night and those who has and will witness its beauty will forever be changed by the wonder it brings. I hope that you will ask the question when you find the moments that makes you wonder. If the sky is not a sky then what is it?

Everything becomes harder to comprehend with each step because of the anxiety which doubt creates. Even here despite all I knew I was struggling to let go of some of the old. Some things are so much harder to let go of than others but as I began to see what I could not see before the value became my motivation to continue. The power of this raises questions and grappling with this reality I wondered could I let go of everything, absolutely everything? Could I give the command that shatters the world as other dwellers had done long ago? I believed I could but could I really? Could you take the decision that shatters the comfort of your own world? As time goes by these questions will keep re surfacing because there is no getting away from it. Answering them often leaves you feeling alone with no one to talk too. There is a lot that I miss from before. It changes things and once you know a thing you know it forever. It takes time to come to terms with all the changes. Whilst I am always in good company sometimes I get lonely, it is a human condition, a reminder of the game of life, like the thorns and rose. Loneliness is a feeling, to feel is why this world was created, it does not exist in the timelessness of infamy. Cultivate this feeling. The way it tunnels into us all allows room to grow but do not expect to simply outgrow loneliness. Never hope to find people who will understand you, someone to fill that space, you are that space. With expectation you will only find disappointment for expectation is the root of all heartache. The best you'll do is understand yourself, know what it is that you want, and not let the stones block your way though you will encounter many through this journey of light. It helps thanking oneself for being courageous. People rarely realize that courage comes from the Middle English (denoting the heart, as the seat of feelings) from Old French *corage*, from Latin *cor* 'heart'.

In the Quran it reads… *"Because they are sincere, they are also courageous. For the good pleasure of Allah, they adopt the manners taught by the Qur'an and strive to persuade others to do the same not remaining silent in the face of evil acts committed around them. They take on the responsibility of struggling against evil, and speaking of truth, beauty and virtue. As for the courageous acts of unbelievers, these are carried out solely for their own gain or other worldly ambitions. Therefore, those who are removed from the light of the Qur'an apply what they deem as courage to the wrong situations. In matters where true courage is required, they may actually falter. As such, the courage they usually exemplify is of little purpose, and of no benefit to themselves, with regards to the Hereafter. Being bound by his conscience, a believer cannot fail to be courageous. For example, if an innocent person is accused, and he is aware of his innocence, he defends the person, for the good pleasure of Allah, even if it is in conflict with his own interests, or places him at risk. This is a true example of outstanding courage.*

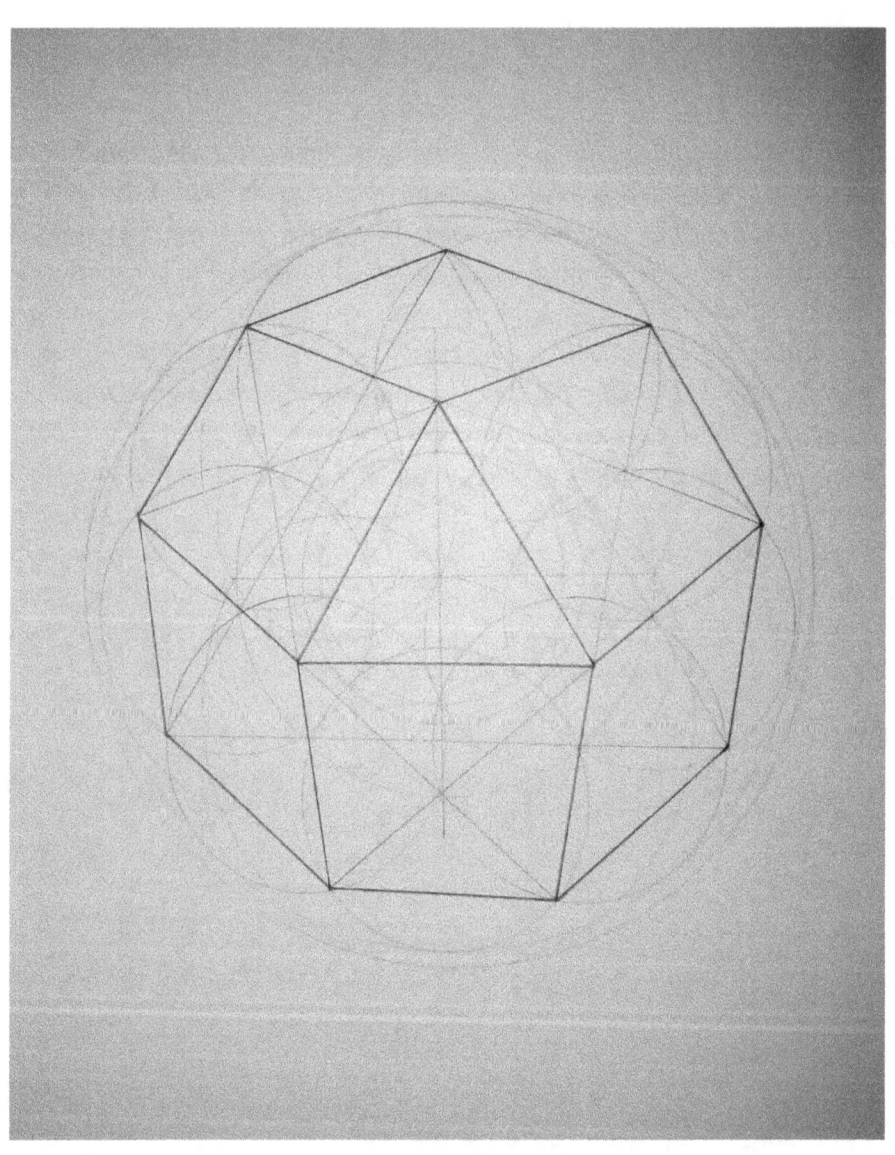

The power of nine can only be known when you know there is nine and that zero and nine is equally the same.

The source of this courage exemplified by the faithful." Sometimes true courage can be found in the most unlikely places by the most unlikely persons that never thought courage existed within them. Such a person who listens to the voice of their conscience and defends the rights of the downtrodden may be asked questions like… "Is it your job to defend him or her?" in an attempt to belittle them and cause them to give up. The truth, however, is that what they are doing is a noble example of morality which deserves appreciation. If the person being criticized also fails to adhere to the morality within, they will be unable to withstand the criticism of those around them and be inclined to their own selfish interest and retaliations. But, if this person has the light within, they never hesitate in implementing the morality commanded of them. This person listens to his conscience and has the courage to fight for justice, even under the most difficult circumstances. When they encounter a wrong, they try to counter it with virtue. For this reason, they may be accused of being naïve and resented by those who do not follow the morality of the light. We can only know who we are when tested and what we do in those moments defines who we are and what we a capable of.

Seeing into the beyond

"DEEP IN THE FINITE THE INFINITE EXISTS" *The Emerald Tablets. "Deep in the hall grew a flower, flaming, expanding, drawing backward night. Placed in its center a ray of great potency, life giving, light giving filling with power all who came near it (your inner Sun)" For the seeker* this is what matters, a part of the code that allows for the question to be asked. This space has been lost in the unrecorded mystery of time and those who once walked where we do. A reminder to all that have wondered and still wonders, to see beyond and remember if only just for a moment the ever changing all silent flame.

Apply pressure when your eyes are closed using your thumbs directly on your pupils. You will experience discomfort behind the eyes (you will know the discomfort when you experience it) hold in

this position for as long as you are willing and have your experience, this may need to be repeated several times. It will take a few minutes to experience so try to be patient. I cannot tell you what happens in that space or else you will manifest it.

Know that you are all things even the most beautiful rose casts a shadow. If there is darkness in you, this darkness may present itself in this space, I believe if you are reading this you are ready to face that darkness and release it. You can find the truth and be one with all of that moment. Take this knowing and begin to see the world lost to the ages cast away into the abyss by the free will of man. See what lay inside of you and try to explain what it all means. When you remove your thumbs or fingers don't open your eyes immediately. Keep them closed for an equal time as you applied pressure longer, if needed. Depending on who you truly are you may only have a momentary glimpse into the beyond, maybe not even and hence you may require several tries. You may need to do some work in this world releasing whatever is inside unlocking the path to the beyond.

I found this space after the many releases shown to me by the guides from within so it is impossible to know what your first attempt will manifest. I couldn't account for what it was and it took a long time to understand that space, what it meant and how its operations worked. Only when I began to understand myself did it make more sense. At the time the collective experience was overwhelming and this effect boosted the cause allowing me to continue taking that moment being vulnerable. To consider fear and its mechanisms, to lay down the sedatives, weapons and defenses- one at a time, to pursue this new knowing with my open heart. What I saw there changed everything for me, only you can determine the effect it has on you should you choose.

In the Tablets it reads... *'Rolled back swiftly the curtain of darkness, unveiled the hall from the darkness of night. Then grew in the space before me flame after flame from the veil of the night. Uncountered millions leaped they before me some flaming forth as flowers of fire, others there were that shed a dim radiance flowing but faintly from out of the night. Some there were that faded swiftly, others that grew from a small spark of light. Each surrounded by its dim veil of darkness, yet flaming with light that could never be quenched. Coming and going like fireflies in the springtime, filled they the space with light and with life."* When you have experienced the space where the eternal flame glows for some, darkness may come for others. Flashes, sparkles, squares and geometry. Depending on your experience maybe difficult and challenging. Like the geometry if you don't experience anything it speaks to a deep disconnection with oneself and spirit. For those who have had the experience with me have had varying results. Remember the absence of light is also a color. Here is where the soul resides and the true fire. Whatever your experience you can explore it in that space without fear or judgement. You are the only judge. Use it as a means to access the light body. From the book of Matthew it is quoted…*"When the eye is single your whole body will be full of light…"* It is your living proof that we are all united. I'm not sure how stanch religions will accept this when their principle structures are based on salvation through the institution they represent and not through the self. Regardless the truth is still the truth, your soul is your own, it always has been and it always will be.

Religion whether good or bad should serve as a guide only and not as a mandatory mechanism to whatever salvation they offer. This is verified from the book of Thomas where *Jesus said…"If those who lead you say to you, see, the kingdom is in the sky then the birds of the sky will precede you. If they say to you it is in the sea then the fish will precede you. Rather, the kingdom is inside of you, and it is outside of you. When you come to know yourselves, then you will become known, and you will realize that it is you who are the sons of the living father. But if you will not know yourselves, you dwell in poverty and it is you who are that poverty."*

Religion comes from the Latin word religiare, to bind. So the meaning of religion at least literally is to create a bond with the All. Religion is a fundamental set of beliefs and practices generally agreed upon by a group of people concerning the cause, nature, and purpose of the universe, and involve devotional and ritual observances. They also contain a moral code governing the conduct of human affairs. The whole purpose of religion is to facilitate love and compassion, patience, tolerance, humility, and forgiveness. It is a path towards truth which at times one has to go alone finding one's own way. You cannot follow another, you cannot move on a beaten path. The more you search your own path, the closer you will be to the All. Jesus summarized the true meaning of religion in Matthew 22:37-40, "Love the Lord your God with all your heart and with all your soul and with all your mind. Love your neighbor as yourself." Religion is realization of the unity of life. In verse 11 of Chapter 4 of Bhagavad Gita, the Lord says... "With his infinite love, that it does not matter what religion you profess." See yourself as an incomplete rainbow with more colors than you may think. Rainbows are mysterious like our thoughts, woven together with water, air and angles of sunlight in all their platonic beauty. To me they are a hidden message in plain sight like the moon..."*The universe is a Mystery and you're part of it, you are it.*" For some that is all the answer that is needed, for others an explanation is required so if you have experienced a music of colors they are your energy fields or chakras, the light that creates the experience of self. If you have seen white only with greyish black shapes like the white noise on a TV though not as pronounced this is chaos / order the outer realms of the human dual experience (a deeper understanding here will be required, look within for the answer and you will find it). See it as a position of the absence of awareness. You have come down from the clouds to the inner earth and unwind grounding yourself and being one with the great mother. This opens the pathway. There are other ways but this is the right way. Know if you are bound you will see it there. It will look unnatural and you will feel it. *'Mighty beyond words is the flame of the Cosmic, hanging in planes, unknown to man. Mighty and balanced, moving in order, music of harmonies, far beyond man. Speaking with music, singing with color, flame from the beginning of Eternity's ALL. Spark of the flame art thou, O my children, burning with color and living with music. List to the voice and thou shalt be free. Consciousness free is fused with the Cosmic, one with the Order and Law of the*

ALL. Knew ye not man, that out of the darkness, Light shall flame forth, a symbol of ALL."

Use your hands for they are a representation of the outer world. The left hand thumb being zero and right hand thumb being nine. The same applies to your feet, they are a representation of your inner world with the left small toe is zero and right small toe is nine. The human body holds many mysteries. When you begin to access your inner energies you'll notice temperature changes in your hands and feet. Extremely cold is too much radian flow (divine energy is cold) too warm is too much resistance. You want a comfortable room temperature. This is the zero point you are searching for.

It may sound weird and simple but coming to know this was impossibly difficult and took a very long time to understand before it could be communicated. For many it may be over active, some of you may actually need to lower your vibration whilst some may need to increase it in search of your zero point of the true self. This is where the vertigo can be an issue and this works both ways. Know this is part of the process along with palpitations, sweating, getting hot then cold, flashes of light, blurry vision especially specific focused blur centered. Goosebumps, ringing and blocked ears at strange times, feeling like you are under water, hair standing on end. Also strangely headaches and flashes are very common signs of rapid shifts like tuning from one radio station to another.

Spending time in nature helps. Everything natural has in it the spirit of life and has its own vibration when you look at something long enough with the right vibration, angle and intent you bind frequencies and connect with that thing. Green is the heart and green is the key. You will have to learn the blinking rate for connection, this requires practice with the eyes and can be very difficult. You will know your default vibration because when you try not blinking your eyes will burn that's the limits of your default. For me overcoming this has taken years and I'm still learning. I can tell you that the right mindset will automatically adjust the blink ratio. This applies to everything that has the divine code in it. Try it with the stars you may experience when looking at stars that it's hard to focus on one as if it's moving from left to right or right to left. This has nothing to do with your eyes, the dark or depth perception. If you are not allowed to communicate on a specific vibration then you will need to release within to create the flowing vibration resulting in the connection. Try the alignment angles using the pyramid as I spoke of. The same applies to all the platonic solids. Using the geometry and a still mind initially will help unlock the code inside, remember to see the geometry as yourself. Use the rising and setting sun, it is cool enough not to hurt the eyes and the angles match without too much adjustment on the part of the person, once the crown chakra is open it serves as a UV protector or at least to me it feels that way. In the Tablets it reads *"Free, let thine soul soar ever upward, free from the bondage and fetters of night. Lift thine eyes to the Sun in the sky-space. For thee, let it be a symbol of life. Know that thou art the Greater Light, perfect in thine own sphere when thou art free."* The sun's rays holds the divine code and must be used to activate the light body when you are present in purpose, hold your eyes as if you had three and align it as one with a level head and the eyes angled upward, just look at it and enjoy the moment without blinking for as long as you can. The colors and effects are your own to answer based on your position of mind.

Consider developing a set of affirmations as stated before aligned with the platonics and the forces they represent being consistent in the application of the natural way. This alignment will aid the release of anything that does not serve your wellness. (*To give you an idea, any routine based comfort or habit must be released. So if you like mayonnaise you are going to have to stop eating mayo and replace it with something that naturally helps and serves your wellness*). Suppression comes in many forms. Check your resistance levels vs your tolerance levels. Tolerance can be a mechanism of suppression. I have spoken of this in the book earlier, it is of the utmost importance to understand.

Treat this information with respect and patience. Do not use it on another that may not be ready to experience it, it has far reaching consequences. If the other has darkness in them they may find irreversible chaos. Opening the light body is strenuous on the physical body. You may need to get into a bit of shape first depending on your physical condition. This is not a joke so take it seriously this journey in part is like an exorcism where you are the priest, the demon and the person being exorcised. There is a reason why you have become what you are. The law of cause and effect works both ways. Thus improving in health aligns with the improvement in spirit when you are aware of spirit and not getting into shape to serve your Ego. Do remember… *"seek not that which is not of the law, for such exists only in the illusion of the sensors"*…*Emerald Tablets.*

Open your eyes for the first time

We can so easily blind ourselves never seeing what was right in front of us because we never think to look there as we perceive problems to be too great to be that simple and close- so it becomes the perfect place to hide. When we rectify this then we can see the world with eyes filled with the light of love. Eyes clear of the stains of the past washed away by the tears of purpose. With all that had transpired I was finally free from the old way. I never thought I would be able to forgive and let go of the hatred and bitterness. It was no longer in me and I wasn't angry anymore. Revenge was no longer a part of me.

A new day had been born, my first for a very long time. Starring at the sun of the morning I made my commitment to resolute all the imbalances left inside of myself. To give the words I've written in this book life. For the first time I felt like I could face a day without pretending to be me. I had never known true strength I grew up too quickly to learn. I didn't have time to be a boy. I didn't have a choice but to be strong, to overcome fear despite how afraid I was. To find courage when I didn't have any. To give when I had nothing left inside. To motivate and inspire when I was broken and destroyed. To serve a duty without question and defend what I didn't understand. That me I had been set free.

This was my smile that I never showed before, for once I was really okay. For once I found a reason to hope, real hope and the power to believe in myself. I chose a better way and I was proud of myself for doing so. I chose to be a leader, I chose to forgive and retire my weapons because I didn't need my defenses anymore. That day something changed in the sun. It was brighter than I had ever seen before as if a light in me turned on because a light in me did turn on. I was overwhelmed, these were tears of goodness. I didn't know where here was and it didn't matter because I was free of the need to control and it felt so good to think this way. Life's was so hard, I didn't always know the way so anyway would do at times. I was alone and afraid for so long and I would turn to anything for comfort. Many times I turned to the darkness without realizing what I was giving myself to it because I needed comfort from life's storms, anything to face that pain alone. Whatever the poison to numb the suffering that comes with pain. In truth I had to die many times over by my own will so I could be reborn in this life free of

death. *"Death but not as you know death but a death that is light and is life."* A new me and a new now. A better expression of myself aligned with the cosmos and the knowing of the light within. I may have chosen to be here and so I was strong enough to face this life alone but it would be nice to have a helping hand that does not have any intentions other than to help. Whilst I never always had it I could be that helping hand to someone. In that moment a voice vibrated in silence…"We can all be that helping hand to another." It is the truth. I have chosen to rise from here with the power of goodness. Life taught me how little I needed to be happy and how much I needed to cover up that I wasn't.

I now understood the lesson and the instructions from the tablets and it resonates with all texts… *"Saw I the moldings of Order from the chaos and angles of night. Saw I the LIGHT, spring from Order and heard the voice of the Light. Saw I the flame of the Abyss, casting forth Order and Light. Saw Order spring out of chaos. Saw Light giving forth Life. Then heard I the voice. Hear thou and understand. The flame is the source of all things, containing all things in potentiality. The Order that sent forth light is the WORD and from the WORD, COME LIFE and the existence of all. And again spoke the voice saying: THE LIFE in thee is the WORD. Find thou the LIFE within thee and have powers to use of the WORD. Long I watched the Light-flame, pouring forth from the Essence of Fire, realizing that LIFE but Order and that man is one with the fire. Back I came to my body stood again with the Nine, listened to the voice of the Cycles, vibrate with powers they spoke: Know ye, O Thoth, that LIFE is but thee WORD of the FIRE. The LIFE forth ye seek before thee is but the WORD in the World as a fire. Seek ye the path to the WORD and Powers shall surely be thine. Then asked I of the Nine: O Lord, show me the path. Give the path to the wisdom. Show me the way to the WORD.* Answered, me *then, the* LORD OF THE NINE: **Through ORDER, ye shall find the way. Saw ye that the WORD came from Chaos? Saw ye not that LIGHT came from FIRE? Look in thy life for this order. Balance and order thy life. Quell all the Chaos of the emotions and thou shalt have order in LIFE. ORDER brought forth from Chaos will bring thee the WORD of the SOURCE, will thee the power of CYCLES, and make of thy Soul a force that** *freewill extend through the ages, a perfect SUN from the Source. <u>Listened I to the voice and deep thanked the words in my heart</u>. Forever have I sought for order that I might draw on the WORD. Know ye that <u>he who attains it must ever in ORDER be for use of the WORD</u> though this order has never and can never be. Take ye these words, O man. As part of thy life, let them be. Seek thee to conquer this order and One with the WORD thou shalt be.* Put forth thy effort in gaining LIGHT on the pathway of Life. Seek to be One with the SUN/state. Seek to be solely the LIGHT. Hold thou thy thought on the Oneness of Light with the body of man. Know that all is Order from Chaos born into light."

If this sounds cryptic and confusing then simply start by introducing yourself to all of the universe. Announce your arrival in goodness and purpose remembering the law of truth. These instructions may appear too fantastical to even consider as plausible. For me it was impossible to perceive once and required many veils to be lifted first. I was never looking to find a map in the stars, I didn't even know to look for it. This journey was designed to right the wrongs of my history, removing the toxic and become a happier healthier human being that cared more and was willing to show it, it still is. This is how I discovered the gateway to the stars.

When I look back on the years where I started questioning my humanity many times I found myself shattered and hopeless. I am not shattered anymore. I am becoming the liquid crystal image of infinite change. This is my flower moving and spinning to the tune of my vibration, that is what we do, that is what every petal in the flower does. Each of us are a product of the differential pressure acting on the three stages of self as either a particle or wave or both collectively making up the whole. Seek the harmonious triple point where all phases of self exists simultaneously. Physical, mental and astral. It is not an impossible state to achieve. But it's close to impossible. I'll say this..."*In my life I knew something was out of place. If I never chose to act on that thought I'd not have known how deep inward it is possible to go.*" Regardless of my failings and I am more grateful today more than I was yesterday and that means a lot to me. For once I'm living without shame, without the fear of my heart shutting down as it did before. I can smile because I enjoy it and I enjoy sharing it with those around me. I enjoy doing right by the wisdom I know today. Sharing the knowledge to all who seeks it. Knowledge should always be free to the seeking and the willing. Knowledge must never be kept idle. It must always be applied so that the light of wisdom may continue to grow. We are good people inside when we choose to be. Time may have eroded our spirit but our spirits are infinite. The path to it is always there should you wish to find your way home. There is no one who knows you better than you. All guides are manifestations of you designed to show you the way. The guides in your life can be called many things but they are still a part of the oneness of self. *"Know ye that the Lords of the Cycles are units of consciousness sent from the others to unify this with the All. Highest are they of the consciousness of all the Cycles, working in harmony with the Law. Know They that in time all will be perfected, having none above and none below, but all One in a perfected Infinity, a harmony of all in the Oneness of All"* Emerald Tablets

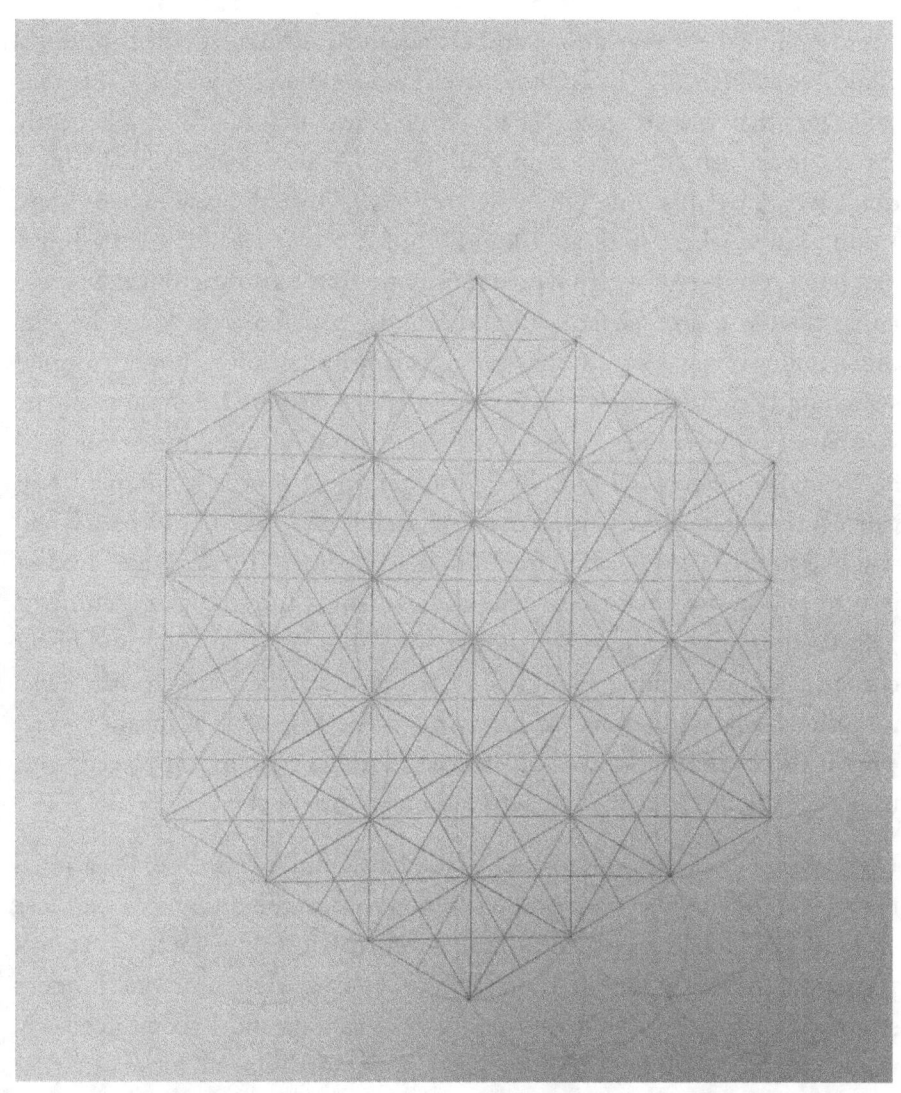

See the angles and the curves as the union of worlds makes up the all of the all. Each has its purpose. Each has its place. One in the other yet not in the other.

What is worth fighting for?

Amidst all of these revelations and changes one evening a voice appeared while I was in bed. I had come to know the energies within. This was different, this was a voice I had never heard before. A simple softly spoken word caught my attention…"Hello" I answered "Who is this I don't recognize this tone" the voice replied…"I don't know where I am. I don't know where here is" I knew who the voice was. The little boy I had been searching for this whole time. I tried to be strong but it was too hard when you are speaking to the original you. I always knew he was there, I never gave up even when I had nothing left I never stopped searching because I knew there was more. I whispered…"You are safe, you have nothing to fear. You are free and you don't need me anymore, I am ready to go now all is well" It was the most powerful moment you can ever imagine. I got up, went downstairs and asked…"What would you like to do?" and I said softly "I'm going home. You are free." I burst into tears because I felt free. Of all the hardships endured in a lifetime of pain there is always a part that hopes for a moment that for some never comes. After everything I had been through I watched myself drift away into the eternal night. I would lie trying to describe what it meant to me. That is the word, true power of silence. That night the moon placed itself in my eyes as the stars moved across the dark bright sky.

I felt like the great hound bowing to the hawk and it was time. I searched through all of the heavens and hells trying to find the little boy I had lost so long ago. I had never met him, never got to know him. I was too young when I lost him. I didn't know how to find him but I never stopped looking. I didn't need to ask any questions and I didn't need any more answers. I didn't need to hold onto anything anymore. In that moment I released a lifetime of struggle to know this freedom and the peace it put in my heart. Of all the things that happened on this journey none was more special than the gift of love I gave myself.

I could finally rest and heal. A part of me wanted to leave that evening too and say goodbye to this world because my journey was completed. The war was finally over. Should have chosen too, there would have been no fault. I was in control of my destiny. But that night I remembered what was said long ago when my heart told me about another journey. I wasn't done yet. I could learn more and share what I've learnt with the world so we may remember who we truly are. We are witnesses to the dawn of a new era in consciousness, at the beginning of this age. We begin the path to unity away from this duality that has kept us separated from our divine right. To remember and KNOW that the light has always been inside of us because we are the light. Even in our dying breath we will know that we are the master of death as we are equally the master of our own life. The tablets taught me this… *"When he have learnt that nothing but the progress of soul can count then he are truly free to work in a harmony with law"* I had unlocked the gateway to infinity's heart. A new dimension of being and there were more lessons to come. Knowledge is and always will be infinite. The goal now is the striving toward excellence in all aspects of self like the diamond. This is the true alchemical pursuit from the light in the dark and the perfection of the soul, gold is but a stepping stone on the great path. The impossible journey with or without the light through the time of the children of man. The light became the faith I built on day after day as I evolved into the new way.

I found this harmony inside of myself. I never thought it was possible. Now I treat myself with the patience and kindness the way I always wanted someone to treat me and I do my best to treat others the same without enablement. I knew I could make it last and I continue ever onward toward the unknown because some moments are worth fighting for. Even in failure I learnt the most precious lessons and with it I began expanding into plains that remains unknown today. I got to see inside areas within the construct that lay deep within the first circle. Beautiful states of mind that reflects in perfect geometric order. I now know they can only exist when one reaches the position of consciousness it represents. I began spending more time doing the things I grew to love moving further away from the old finding joy in watching my roses grow. Learning to partake in the power of the water and sun, the wind and rain. Learning how much water we as humans need and learning its true power. Living close to and at times in balance and seeing that balance breathing in my growing light opening new pathways with new colors. I grew brighter when my knowing caught up to my exploring. I began trusting my intuition. Standing up for what was right, praising goodness and motivating a better way. I learnt to trust myself and my judgment passing the tests the guardians bring in the pursuit of balance.

I started resisting even less as I began my new journey to nowhere. There are times I am nervous, I am still human but I'm working on it. One step dear reader is all it takes. I have decided to ask new questions. Now I understand why I'm doing it, that's what has changed. I will say that it isn't easy to just let go and that's my lesson to learn. To trust absolutely, it will also be your lesson to learn should you partake in this beautiful madness. I have wondered through the many spaces of my mind searching for what began as a broken heart in the darkness where buried souls lay, lost and alone. I was afraid and in pieces. I'm not broken anymore. I have restored my faith in myself and my faith in the universe and its every changing way. I have found peace in the unpredictability of the movement of energy and flow more with it these days. I became the Dweller inside, mastering darkness but still not mastering dancing.

I am okay to be alone these days. No one can know their own beauty or perceive a sense of their own worth until it has been reflected back in the mirror. The mirror is a reflection of truth for those willing to look long enough. I choose truth, I don't settle for the nonsense or the false peace as I used to. I correct myself when I'm wrong and I correct others pretending to be right. I choose to share testing first to ensure the great wisdom is not lost to false causes. In goodness I hope that it may connect the channels for those who listens to it.

As we begin to see deeper than ever before we come closer to the twelve and the one. Knowing is the key to the expansion inward you seek.

The gift is the purpose found after the awakening and it is a worthy pursuit. Seeing oneself blending with the all in ways you can't imagine and that's how you will know it's real. The universe will always be mathematical in its precise nature until it isn't. It is simply beautiful, get to know yourself and your purpose. Allow yourself to make mistakes and grow from it. The more you give the more the universe gives you. Know that you are Moon, shining bright in the darkest night. You are the balance that holds yourself in your orbit which prevents you from spinning into madness. Be a pillar of strength and stability to the world around you, find the three way path of the balance where the light breathes, it is unmistakable and will change all that you know.

I ask you what you will do with eternal life and the freedom it brings. What will you do when you know the truth of who you are? Will you become a light in this world? Take up the striving and build greater laws where wisdom leads? Will you have the courage to expose yourself and live in the highest truth only? You have a choice to make this world a better place but you have the free will to do nothing, to be as you always were, remember… *"that ever receding thy goals shall elude thee from day unto day"*

Do not give yourself to the unnatural way, do not be controlled by half-truths and whole lies. Do not settle for the dogma of old, do not give yourself to blood sacrifice and mysticism. This is not the way, the ancient texts says the keys lay in the blood of the youth, this doesn't mean cutting up people or children. Find the youthful blood inside yourself. Cure the imbalance of your inheritance and impedance. This is the true meaning of the ancient texts. Many of the old texts has been jaded by false perception, agenda and circumstance. Love is life, see if your actions reflect love? Ask yourself "If the whole world was doing what I am now would I be happy with the world I'm creating?" See the effect of the cause of your actions. Nothing is new in this universe. *"In all space there is only one wisdom, though seemingly decided it is one in the one, all that exist come forth from the light and the light comes forth from the all, everything that is created is based upon order, law rules the space where the infinite dwells"* Emerald Tablets

All the ancient texts may speak the same but they cannot show you what you won't see. Remove the veils of separation as I have spoken of, forget everything you've been taught and become your own teacher, forget the words of this book should it be required. See the flower of life for what it truly is. Remove every circle after and ask yourself, what's left? If you say a blank page or wall then so be it but don't forget you the artist drawing it, the multiverse and the universe is always present flowing through and around you. Comprehend this. It is needed to gauge the gravity of the all.

Without purpose you may never find what you are looking for and you may take anything as what you were looking for. Know… *"They that are guided go not astray but they that are lost cannot find a straight path"* Emerald Tablets. You don't have to sit still for several hours to find answers to the questions that your eyes are giving you, the clues too. Look closely, see what you cannot see right in front of you. Be open to the clues you are showing yourself, be open to the universes' guidance. Prayers are always being answered but you need to know who you are praying to and why. There are no convenient answers, unfortunately the universe is not going to lie.

The light Body

There are many trials of the outer that must be overcome before you can find the light body inside. Below points compresses some of the writings in this book relating to the various energy meridians. Use it as your guide.

"Master the seven and take it from there. Know that there are more than seven but without the seven the rest wouldn't matter as they cannot be accessed before the seven has been activated and ordered. Make your own list, be present with all of you the good and the bad. Do not ignore either, energy does not exist without purpose. Your true purpose is not to make you rich (but then most assumes rich equals how much money

you have). The false self makes with this assumption. Just remember all the money in the world won't buy you an extra five minutes with your loved ones when the stress of the life you chose attacks your body and your dying breath is one of regret and remorse."

I am (1) EARTH HEXAHEDRON

- You will have to make peace with the fact that you are not human
- You will have to reset your inner knowing of yourself
- You will have to align yourself with who your parents actually are
- You will have to know that you have chosen to be here
- You will have to face all your fears and release all of the unknown (uncharted)
- You must know you are strong enough to face anything because you are everything
- Think less and act more in alignment with law

I feel (2) WATER ICOSOHEDRAON

- Become your own judge – judge honestly and fairly
- Raise up what you suppress
- Don't hold back, resistance is telling yourself there is something out of place
- Check your habits (wearing make-up is a habit ladies, you are beautiful and you are perfect as you are, find the beauty within that does not require cover ups.)
- How you treat everyone is a reflection of how you treat your inner self
- Know the law

- Express the truth even if it gets you in trouble
- Align yourself with the 42 virtues of MA'AT (or whatever your culture holds as the highest virtues)
- Align your expression with the law
- Release the desires of the body by outletting your sexual energy into creative energy, see the power that comes from sharing here.
- Develop patience and tolerance here.

I will (3) FIRE TETRAHEDRON

- What are you using you fire for?
- Do you incline towards a negative mind? Here you must be absolutely honest.
- Inspire your yourself
- Motivate those around you because they are you
- Be the change in your own life, talk less and observe before you engage.
- Be more kind, grateful and compassionate- these cools the mighty fire and stills the soul
- Here you want to cool the fire, not extinguish but give rise to the true fire within. MIRROR

I love (4) LOVE (POLE SHIFT) STAR TETRAHEDRON

- Love is the force that overcomes all, the true creative energy
- Love is always kind, it is never blind or deaf.
- Love isn't silent in the presence of hate, yet treats hate with love not with hate

- Love is not enablement
- Love is not happiness that masks pain
- Love is not BIAS
- If your heart is broken you can never love and so everything comes from below, below is negative, freedom cannot be found here.
- When you are below you do not know you are below
- The pole shift is noticeable and you will know when you have opened the true heart
- Sometimes love may appear cruel when the rectification comes from the darkness where love sometimes must go to free itself, (those who argue with you may care more for you than those who do nothing)

I speak (5) AIR OCTAHEDRON

- Take note of the words you use.
- How do you speak of yourself? Do you lie about who and what you are?
- Words create binding spells, learn to speak without binding yourself.
- Do you even speak at all?
- Watch your inner dialogue. Do you curse people in your silence?
- Do you speak about wisdom you do not have?
- Do you say things you cannot validate?
- Do you stand up for things you know are wrong?
- Start speaking only the truth no matter the consequences you perceive
- Ask for forgiveness
- Find the path to the WORD and the POWER

I see (6) ETHER DODECAHEDRON

- What is it you choose to ignore?
- What is it you deny?
- What do you avoid?
- Here you can see the connection between the above and below.
- Here you must open your eyes to the cold hard reality of absolute truth
- What choices have you made and why have you made those choices?
- E.g. why are you over weight?
- E.g. your wife or husband is cheating on you, why do you look the other way?
- E.g. your health is deteriorating, why are you still eating and living so unhealthy
- E.g. your house is a mess, why do you tell others to clean their houses yet you don't clean your own?

I understand (7) SPHERE

- I understand that I am responsible for my happiness and my life
- I am responsible for the happiness of those around me
- I understand that we is stronger than I
- I understand that I must make changes to either improve or hurt myself
- I understand that it is hard work and I am willing to put in that hard work

- E.g. I understand that I talk a lot of nonsense sometimes and I'm going to rectify that

- E.g. I understand that I can be a better person/husband/father, I can be a human being

- E.g. I understand that I'm selfish and I can share more

- E.g. I understand that my room is a mess and I have no excuse not to clean it.

These are the initial trials to be overcome. It sounds simple but it isn't. The mind must be reset. Every last piece of the inside must be observed, assessed, balanced and ordered in alignment with the law. The inner activation requires the combination of the release and replacement of the original light codex that comes from the sacred geometry. The journey inward will break you and it must until you give birth to what must come. The space behind the eyes will tell you the condition of your light. You will need to bring that space into the space when your eyes are just closed and then should you will bring it to this world. That requires a more aggressive routine of release and is more disciplined in its ritualistic nature. This allows you to hold the moment as you strive toward the zero point wave. You must be in a state of fight or flight and you must rise above the need to fight then you can take flight into the dimensions beyond. Holding your eyes fixed is important as it will show you the dimensions as you become one with the vibrations you don't know yet exists. You will need to elevate the heart's rate, not sleeping here helps. You can use stimulants but note there may be consequences and these consequences are very real. Beware because madness dwells inside as the light does equally.

I used the moon, stars, sky and clouds, holding my vibration as explained, keeping all of me open. This allowed the light of the universe to pour in through my eyes using only the curves and, began to grow the flame within. I held my thoughts in these spaces and the guides showed me the way until I was given the key to enter on my own. When the self is no longer influenced by the ways of the old, the silence one requires is readily available. Know on this journey I didn't give much time to mainstream mediation and whilst it has its purpose I chose instead a different method. I focused on a singular thought and held that thought till this day, that thought is the light that was molded from the darkness of Night. That is the power of love.

When you begin to experience light flashes and colors, here you will know that there is order to it as I spoke of. The sacred geometry serves as star gates to allow bridging the gap between this world and the other, think of the geometry as the programmer and the program that must be loaded into your consciousness to activate the pathways of the light body. Initially you will find you have a lot of resistance as you will see little results. You must persevere.

Remember the angle of 15deg. Remember heart rates exceeding 105bpm. In my journey I got my heart rate up as high as 245bpm and as low as 39bpm. 39 is a code in itself, F – 6, R – 9, E – 5, E – 5, D- 4, O – 6, M – 4 = 39. I believe it was the intention of the $E=mc^2$ equation to show us this. If not then it is an amazing coincidence, as M at 90deg is 3 and C squared is 9 with E being the zero point at 5. (Dimensional shifts by the ancients are at 90deg, I didn't use it in Freedom because freedom is pre-dimensional shift). When you look at the varying alpha numerical breakdowns you will see many numbers repeating. Like EARTH, put the H at the beginning and it spells HEART. When we include the sun earth is the 4th position in our system as is the heart being the 4th chakra. You will go on to find all the seeming coincidences and you will have to question why? Equally a skeptic can pass such things off as nonsense. It is your free will to determine your own cause. As stated before step aside and allow others to rise. Your choice must never hurt another.

Be patient, this journey takes years not days and your commitment through the dark will determine whether you find the light within. The heart must be free first before you make the shift through the mirror that binds you to the lower chakras. There will be moments where you are quietly motivated from inside to do things like look at stars and the moon, go into nature or the ocean. Do not ignore the signs they have purpose. Follow your intuition, this can be hard when there is many selves within the whole. It becomes easier when you develop your own Master References which is aligned with the law.

In That space behind your eyes you are looking for the music of color blending with spiraling fire that flows in the center. *"He who know that the fire is within himself shall ascend unto the eternal fire and dwell in it eternally, Fire the inner fire is the most potent of all force for it overcomes all things and penetrates to all things of the earth."* Emerald Tablets. Use the book as a guide to understand the colors and read through my words as reference, they are layered just like the tablets and for the true seeker will see the deeper meanings. I must apologize but it has to be this way. When you remove the hands off the eyes with the eyes closed you are looking for an overwhelming light.

You will know when you find the spaces I have spoken of because your eyes will change the way you see. A haze of movement that appears to distort the image of normal reality. Initially there will be no color, only movement like 2 circles overlapping yet flowing opposite to each other or not. Read up about the merkaba and know Mer – Ka – Ba is a 3 step journey like the triangle. Think of this example, if you take a circle and turn it 90deg it becomes a straight line. This journey is looking at the mind from that perspective.

The light body when active moves on multiple dimensional orbitals which your thoughts and diet, exposure to light, dark, water, sun etc. influences, when the light body is active you will see the movements of your light energies reflected in your outer world vision, on the inner world you'll experience this movement when your eyes are closed. We know them as orbs, they are conscious because we are conscious. There are multiple layers of activation remember that 1 orb is not the end. They have layers of colors both individual and combined. There is a vision that extends into an unknown, it lays in the black sun, it is a code not an eclipse, it will change what you understand and change the colors and its order. Individually they form combinations and move in a specific way speeding up or slowing down as you do, as its direction is affected by your vibration, it is deep within the moment without thought that you will see. *"All eyes do not see with the same vision for to one an object appears in one form and color and to a different eye of another, so to also the eternal fire changing from color to color is never the same from day to day"* The Emerald Tablets.

From the Emerald Tablets I learnt many things which I have shared. It has showed me how my thoughts can affect the weather, how I can heal myself. How the pyramids were built and why, the true nature of time in its cyclic beauty. How comet strikes work and collective global events. What happened to the Atlanteans, who the beings of light and Gods of old were. How the "stair step" evolution works which today cannot be accounted for. How the frequencies of the dimensions works and why. How to access them and partake in the wisdom it shares and who is sharing the wisdom. What the flash of light was that I saw and have seen many times since, the gateway that unlocked when one becomes the whole just as the whole is the whole. How to read the maps in the skies with the movements that I once thought was satellites until flashes moved in movements that could not be satellites. Who the hounds were and their purpose. What the many shooting stars meant that would appear at exactly the right moment just like it did the first time but in a different form. How I projected my reality and who the people were in my life was and what purpose they served. Many secrets have been shared along the way. If you want to know what Atlantis was simply look around you, we are Atlantis. Freedom can be found in this lifetime for there is only ever this lifetime repeating separated by the growth of your soul. This determines the growth of your understanding of the law and your ability to work with it. The tablets speak to the true heart and it is the hearts connection to the tablets and the color itself that creates the resonating frequency. I've listened to it and red it more times than I can count. Each time my consciousness grows I hear its words resonate to a different vibration revealing new codex, but listening to it means nothing without application. It's far from done. I've asked this question, has no one else made these connections with the tablets? Has no else uncovered what I have? If they have surely they would've shared it with the world? Why then can't I find any of this knowledge? We have a right to know, we have a right to be free from bondage even if it ends the world so that a new one may begin and perhaps it's time.

We all deserve to know our true heritage. To know that energy always was and always will be. To partake in the beauty of the starry night. If there are forces within our current reality holding the knowledge for their own personal gain then let that come to an end right now, you now have that power. I am aware that it will be difficult initially coming to terms with everything, especially after you see what lays behind your eyes. From there a lot of what may happen will appear beyond strange. Know that it isn't and has to be experienced then you can feel the results as it reveals itself to you through your own self, not imagined but within a higher dimension of expression. As I've stated just because this knowledge is lost to this world, does not mean it doesn't exist. Look to the past and you will see the all the answers when you know that time cycles.

"Know ye, O man, that all of the future is an open book to him who can read. All effect shall bring forth its causes as all effects grew from the first cause. Know ye the future is not fixed or stable but varies as cause brings forth an effect. Look in the cause thou shalt bring into being, and surely thou shalt see that all is effect. So, O man, be sure the effects that ye bring forth are ever causes of more perfect effects. Know ye the future is never in fixation but follows man's free will as it moves through the movements of time-space toward the goal where a new time begins. Man can only read the future through the causes that bring the effects. Seek ye within the causation and surely ye shall find the effects. List ye, O man, while I speak of the future, speak of the effect that follows the cause. Know ye that man in his journey light-ward is ever seeking escape from the night that surrounds him, like the shadows that surround the stars in the sky and like the stars in the sky-space, he, too, shall shine from the shadows of night." Emerald Tablets

I believe that this knowledge is everyone's divine right so I ask again that you treat it respectfully. Knowing the truth, living the truth keeps the heart open – truth is love. Calm the inner voices. Freedom only comes when you have earned your way. Using darkness will only bring further darkness. Become the observer and listen to your inner self. Listen to those that speaks in silence, their words are your own, know the good and the bad. Freedom and bondage comes from all the dwellers inside, this is what I have learnt. This is and is not you and it will be hard to know the difference because all is you. The choice is yours, knowing yourself will allow you to know who you are and who you are not. To attain higher levels of consciousness you will have to lock your new vibration for 30 x3 days to lock the new vibration, 3 to 4days of void space you must pass through, you will know when you in the void it feels weird and you will feel out of place as if nothing makes sense and you've lost some of your memory, spells of vertigo is common for the shift between your vibration and another vibration depending on the frequency differential, imagine if you will a washing machine spinning – there are moments when it spools up or comes down from the spin that it shakes aggressively, liken this to yourself, you don't want to be shaking.

This journey is one of KNOWING, not belief or proof or anything other than KNOWING. When you know a thing, you connect to the divine way when the knowing matches the law, you will feel this through your being and it will guide your way.

There is a prayer in the Tablets. This prayer is a commitment to the change of vibration, you do not need a circle, only honesty. Use it when needed if needed. Create your own prayer and affirmations, as long as it's truthful then it comes from the heart. Use this during your 90 days and change it according to your preference. I have included a variation below the prayer for your reference.

"Seek ye first a place bound by darkness, place ye a circle around about thee, stand erect in the midst of the circle use though this formula and you shalt be free, raise

though hands to the dark space above thee close thine eyes and draw in the light call to the spirit of life through space time using these words and though shalt be free"

"Fill though my body O spirit of Life, fill though my body with the spirit of Light come from the flower that shines through the darkness, come from the halls where the seven lords rule, name them by name I the Seven, three four five, and six seven eight nine. By their names I call them to aid me, free me and save me from the darkness of night: Untanas, Quertas, Chietal, and Goyana, Huertal, Samveta – Ardal. By their names I employ thee, free me from the darkness and fill me with light.

"When ye have done this ye shalt be free from the fetters that bind he cast off the bondage of the brothers of night"

This became my version of it and serve as an affirmation reminder through my journey.

I am the light. In me is all time and space, I remove the veils to see what I truly am. I will to be free from the darkness of night. I will to be free from shadows within. I am free and I choose to be free. I am all things the good and the bad, I make peace with the good and the bad in acceptance of my true being. I forgive myself for the things I know I've done. I forgive those who has hurt me. I release the negative for always and receive my divine right. I thank myself for having the courage to say these words of the highest. I will my heart open that it may flow through all of me, I thank myself. I am free.

"If your words have been truth of the highest then the works begins, know that this process is NOT once off, you must hold this thought forever. Energy is also moving as is your vibration, what you give your thoughts to become you. (This is well known) However the unconscious is the driving force of the hidden vibration and you must live in this space that is your goal making the all ONE…"

You are looking at yourself looking back at you. You are infinite energy, a star amongst stars when you are free.

Every release brings knew knowledge, the knowledge you gain will tempt you to move away from the light. This must never be your goal, your purpose is to become a better human being. A light to yourself and others. I had come to understand this as it was test like every other.

Rise up carefully

I learnt as the time passed on to be more patient in my pursuit of a better me. I would advise on moderating the progress being weary of replacing habits with other habits or losing the desire almost immediately after starting. The body and what is inside will not let go easy. Transitions in all aspects of being should be based on a sloping gradient, allowing time for the whole being to adjust accordingly. *For example* if you set a goal of losing 10kg, set a timeline of 1 year not 4weeks. It allows for lasting vibrational shifts if you are able to set a routine and follow it. When we tune out of the frequency band what holds onto you is released because of the frequency limitations by which the formless are bound by, as long as we stay out of that previous frequency band after. This is best done with patience over time and understanding. We cycle through all wavelengths as part of the energy flow of the light body. What defines us is where our thoughts go to and why vs our alignment with divine law, so beware of the limitations imposed by old programming.

As an example. If your mother abused you and today you are angry with women but you cannot release that anger so you eat to suppress that anger you now have toward women in your life because you cannot face your own mother as the principle. The physical weight and the eating is a secondary symptom of the principle root problem. If you could forgive your mother truthfully which is the root problem the symptom which is the excessive eating falls away paving the way for you to eat healthier and naturally lose weight (raising your vibration) by putting into your body what is needs vs what the parasite needs. You will still need to remain active as the physical weight is as real as the metaphysical weight. Instead of fast food which keeps you in low vibrations you may decide on some broccoli, this is a hard battle and I have fallen many times here. Discipline is the key and requires time and patience. It's the best advice I can give. You may be disassociated from the trauma of the abuse (remember abuse is not just sexual) and so you don't know why you eat and when someone talks to you about it you are triggered to defend yourself against the original trauma, protecting the original mind which is cut off. As such you'll never truly understand why you eat. You must look deeper at the clues. Consider as I did that there are deeper rooted aspects to our behavior we may not be aware of. This I have found by understanding and working through my own self piece by piece and remember until free of the trigger the problem remains. The trigger becomes a Master Reference.

There are more examples I have discovered in my own journey relating to aspects of self. These I discovered when tackling my own health issues. When we use our intuition and connection to spirit for egotistical intent or we ignore it completely we suffer and imbalance of energy between the upper and mid chakras. Post nasal drips, sinusitis becomes the physical manifested illness. The secondary effect as a result of the principle is throat infections, bronchitis etc. It is a cascading effect.

Asthma is a post trauma effect manifested as a form of anxiety / panic attack. A principle problem of the 4th and 5th chakra. I allowed myself to have asthma attacks without using my pumps or medication to assess the effects, whilst they are not exactly the same as anxiety attacks they stem from the similar root. When the heart is free of the grip of fear the body no longer displays the symptoms. Thus the problem is resolved.

For those who deals with mood shifts during monthly cycles take time to observe them. Do not use these states of minds as a means to be rude or nasty, know that your 1st and 2nd chakras are problematic and requires attention before they manifest into more serious conditions related to this region of the body. When one considers the flow and blockage of energy then by unblocking and releasing the excess energy one can reverse the problems encountered. Many of the people I know that shared the experience with me enjoyed improvements in the own cycles. The same applies to those who carry weight around the mid-section, this is because we are living trapped in the gut. This doesn't mean that the higher energies are cut off, it could mean that they are overactive and in need of balancing. We do not understand how to deal with this so we retreat into the safety of the familiar lower chakras as these are the base human position from creation. We can only know these things when we begin to know who we are and release who we are not thus restoring the balance. This is a forgotten truth. In balance no disease can exist so consider your balance carefully.

Many examples can be made when we begin to understand the purpose of the clues being presented to us. Working on ourselves from the inside rectifies the symptomatic manifestation of the physical imbalance on the outside. Know that anything we don't use is taken away. Nothing can exist without purpose. When we choose not to see, when we choose to ignore, we will lose our sight or one's children will inherit poor eye sight. The same applies to all aspects of the human senses and self. That is why you should not use an illness as a means to excuse yourself from bad behavior, activities or priorities. They will manifest in compounded ways, this is the law. Many times we know what's out of place but we mask it intentionally. You cannot hide or run from what's inside and anyone who can see knows and, those who cares enough to speak up are often the ones you remove from your life to protect those secrets. It is ironic that the defense mechanisms of the human is designed to reject such information via dissonance rather than embrace and liberate oneself. Like the glass of black liquid example, when we are darkened by our choices there are tipping points like a wheel spinning on a car will turn the other way at the right speed and light conditions, so to the humans- energy will do the same. We become the effect of our own cause and thus we can change our illness when we change the mind that created the illness. Remember the glass didn't start black. When we return to our alignment frequencies we rectify the imbalance provided the choice came from within. The intention must come from the infected host.

Cannabis can be used as natural frequency rectifier though modern medicine can't explain this. It can also be used to assess the self-based on the high you get will determine how your state of balance is. So if you partake in a bit of cannabis and you feel sleepy it's because you need sleep. This alignment is only temporary and the mind of the host must be purged of whatever is inside to rectify the imbalance permanently. If you are able to achieve this there is no need for seeking treatment in the outside world. If you smoke cannabis just to get high then you will need to detox from it first to understand your true default alignment.

"Consider a world without medication where being honest with yourself can heal you. Put it to the test. When you heal your inner self, your outer self-thrives. You reverse aging, you find you have more energy, when last did you listen to yourself? Consider if you took note of the obvious issues you know you have and worked through them? If you are a diabetic and you are 40 kilograms overweight because of an eating disorder. Let's say you cannot deal with the mind you can deal with the body. Lose the 40 kilos and the diabetes will subside. Don't ignore everything and treat the symptoms because if you reach and cross the tipping point then the solutions become beyond your ability to implement them. Either way you are responsible for your position as I was for mine and I was making some progress."

Knowing all of this may allow you to save your own life or save a life of someone you care about. It saved mine, yet my mother paid for her choices with her life. I wonder if any of us knew that we risk suffering a debilitating end to the death we call life, would we still continue to make the same choices? How about what it does to next generation? *"Consciousness follows the path of that before, or else all would be repetition in vein"* Emerald tablets. Children that suffer with illness are the hardest to deal with because they are born with the trauma of the unknown so they do not know they are the product of the previous generations' unlearnt lessons designed to teach and show that generation what lay within. Parents if you have suffering children search within yourself for the things you keep within. They have a very real effect on the world around you. Rectify it in yourself before the tipping point in your child is reached and you may rectify the imbalance, children mimics their parents and their environment. Remember when the tipping point has been reached the odds are not in your favor and even if you rectify the imbalance it may be too late already. Sometimes the lesson then is to find peace and let go. Sometimes the child is created to allow one to learn this lesson of letting go.

The grief I suffered losing those closest to me became the foundations of the true understanding of what I was experiencing. I never lost anything and yet the pain of loss is still a reality that must be dealt with before we are free. These lessons can be learned without having to endure the suffering that they often come with. Sadly when we are unaware at times the understanding can come too late. Freedom then comes at a high price. It did for me but removing the shadows of what I became in my ignorance cleared the way for a better me to rise above the repeating cycles I was once trapped in like the hawk. I was free from what I had ignored and this brought a calm that I never felt before. For the first time I found a truth worth fighting for because I was starting to understand my true purpose. This was the key that brought me closer to what I was now searching for which led to changes inside of me and had a profound effect that reflected in the world around me.

Find your way

I hope you will find your way to a place where you can forgive yourself for loving the monster who hurt you or for being the monster who hurt another. Forgiving yourself for caring about someone who used you believing that it is all you were worth, setting yourself free from the anger and bitterness inside. You have a choice. Love, fear, hurt and hate are all part of the same whole. This same whole has within it the good and the bad. I found strength in the places of darkness and remembered who I was. I made that strength my center and started to right the wrongs of the old way. Through self-exposure I've turned the narcissism into inspiration. Together as one in the one balance we become unstoppable. Some energies must be released others may need to be banished, some must be balanced but do remember to give yourself a break every once in a while too. Don't take this journey so serious that you miss the beautiful now! There is nothing wrong with having some fun so long as you consider the law of cause and effect. Many times I wanted to rip my hair out and for what? Instead sometimes I remembered to stop and smell the roses. It works- give it a go. Do that thing you've always wanted to do whatever it may be. You are stopping you, just say to all…"We are doing this, everyone get on board!" shout it out aloud, inside and out. Fear may overwhelm you but that is fear's purpose, to bind us into a vibration of emptiness, it has its purpose; everything has its purpose so if you need a few drinks to loosen up then have a few, just remember in the end all you will need is you. Don't hate yourself if you needed a drink or two, know you are doing good and this day you will dance and allow yourself to make a fool of yourself.

Consider the value of that forgotten smile. Like the tablets the true self can only reveal itself when your resistance has lessened. We are better than fear, you are stronger than fear. Why not fill your mind space with the unborn light that one day will shine in all of your creation? Then we can live as we were designed to, free of our history into our divine creative destiny, transmuting this hell to heaven on earth. We can replace the hurt with healing when we incorporate words like:

Gratitude – say thank you more

Kindness – open a door for someone, help someone with their bags, don't make anyone feel guilty

Inspiration – uplift yourself and those around you, start small here- a smile will do,

Hope – I lost my hope in this life and I will tell you it exists in goodness without expectation hope is the most beautiful thing I never knew till I opened up myself to love and released the hurt and fear of pain that chained me forever

Giving – you will never realize the power of giving until you have given from the heart, the hugs I speak of is life giving, LIGHT GIVING

- Sharing – releasing ourselves from selfishness realizing we are all god's children alike and yet unlike, one great big family and we can heal the world when we heal the world within and share that world with each other

- Mercy – showing mercy to those who has hurt us is the greatest gift you can give someone, it is the power that only the heart has.

- Tolerance – being patient to another is a reflection of the way you treat yourself, this allows us to naturally tolerate another cell, still in the process of growth to the ultimate goal

- Motivation – our ability to motivate others aligns with our perceptions of I and WE, together we motivate each other, and apart we motivate ourselves alone.

If we can begin to use these words as part of our vocabulary we begin to change our collective vibration removing the WORD SPELLS we place on ourselves with our distorted speech and thus we change our reality both on a micro and macrocosmic level. Simple solutions have unbelievable effects on oneself. Changing one's perspective of negative allows for a positive reflection of previously negative situations when we begin to learn through the frustrations of failure, it becomes easier because of our understanding of the hidden meanings of why we are frustrated. Why the universe is showing us what it is in the way it is.

Would you allow yourself to become a student? Would you become your own teacher and would you be a good teacher? Would you be willing to cry or has time dried up your tears, has time walled up the remains of the black heart you've discarded? True strength rises from the fires of despair like the triangle. Here is where you burn off who you are not embracing, who you were always born to be and swim in the oceans of fire for always or, fall into the fire and repeat. It's hard to acknowledge one's failings and take the striving to right the wrongs. To expose oneself in pursuit of a better now. I would say that it's worth it, that all your troubles will melt away and you will find all you are searching for, I would also be lying. This is an impossible journey but if you have the will, you will find me inside ready to take your hand and lead you onward. To show you the way, it may be a secret but you are the only key you need. You are the gateway. Activate the code and you will know that I am not who you think I am just like you are not who you think you are. This is the life you find in the flower. The construct of infinity lies within the first circle. When you are ready all you have to do is take that step.

Imagine living free of the cycle of repeatability to exist in peace and balance drawing off earth's force, changing only when earth does? Imagine the beauty of the unification of the energies within unlocking all things and being one with that all. Consider a world without despair and hopelessness, I am not a dreamer and this is something worth considering. Take the journey or don't but don't stand in someone's way who chooses to. Be man or woman enough set them free on the path of goodness. Do not trap them because you choose bondage. Have the courage to let them go that they may rise in their flight to the stars.

There were times I wished everything would just go back to the way it was before I knew what I now know because I had past- the point of the logical. I answered the question and now you have the option to answer it too. Whatever happens the light will always be inside of you. Whilst the fear crippled me and it is powerful, it is not stronger than any one of us. I'll tell you that it can be very frustrating at the best of times and hopeless at the worst of times. It is why the odds are impossible and that's why you will succeed. I had to die to understand this. The strength you need is inside I swear to you. The power of the universe is inside of us all. There is love flowing even in the darkest caverns of the forgotten. These written words hold a vibration that comes from the heart and is proof that we are never alone. We will remember as our reality moves within the spiraling loops of consciousness, ongoing change will always occur. The Zep Tepi must return to rebalance and recreate new experiences. As the flame of the Crystal creation burns through the fires of the alchemy of experience, there comes a time of separation or merge. Like the flame separates the transition metals of consciousness, they who are enlightened move to a higher light due to their accelerated frequency, and the slag, having to return to the raw materials of the void.

May this journey show you who you truly are. Make it simple and you will see, this was the key that was missing in my life. This is the key to the Emerald Tablets, simplicity. It is why it is impossible to decode. In simplicity we find harmony.

I wish you all the very best and hope to see you living in your divine purpose free of the shadows. Free to shine in the etheric ocean of infinities heart.

Wisdoms call

Does not wisdom call out? Does not understanding raise her voice? At the highest point along the way, where paths meet, she takes her stand beside the gate leading into the city, at the entrance, she cries aloud, "To you", O people, I call out. I raise my voice to all mankind. You who are simple, gain prudence. You who are foolish, set your hearts on it. Listen, for I have trustworthy things to say. I open my lips to speak what is right. My mouth speaks what is true, for my lips detests wickedness. All the words of my mouth is just, none of them is crooked or perverse. To the discerning all of them are right, they are upright to those who have found knowledge. Choose my instruction instead of silver, knowledge rather than gold. For wisdom is more precious than rubies and nothing you desire can compare with her, "I wisdom, dwell together with prudence, I possess knowledge and discretion" I hate pride and arrogance, evil behavior and perverse speech. Counsel and sound judgement are mine. I have insight, I have power, by me king's reign and rulers issue decrees that are just. I love those who loves me, and those who seek to find me. Blessed are those who keep my ways. Watching daily at my doors. For those who find me find life, those who fail to find me harm themselves. All who hate me loves death.

The end

May the star in you shine brightly that you may be a light to this world.

Mmap Nonfiction and Academic series

If you have enjoyed *The Day and the Dweller: A Study of the Emerald Tablets* consider these other fine **Nonfiction and Academic books** from *Mwanaka Media and Publishing:*

Cultural Hybridity and Fixity by Andrew Nyongesa
Tintinnabulation of Literary Theory by Andrew Nyongesa
South Africa and United Nations Peacekeeping Offensive Operations by Antonio Garcia
A Case of Love and Hate by Chenjerai Mhondera
A Cat and Mouse Affair by Bruno Shora
The Scholarship Girl by Abigail George
The Gods Sleep Through It All by Wonder Guchu
PHENOMENOLOGY OF DECOLONIZING THE UNIVERSITY: *Essays in the Contemporary Thoughts of Afrikology* by Zvikomborero Kapuya
Africanization and Americanization Anthology Volume 1, Searching for Interracial, Interstitial, Intersectional and Interstates Meeting Spaces, Africa Vs North America by Tendai R Mwanaka
Africa, UK and Ireland: Writing Politics and Knowledge Production Vol 1 by Tendai R Mwanaka
Writing Language, Culture and Development, Africa Vs Asia Vol 1 by Tendai R Mwanaka, Wanjohi wa Makokha and Upal Deb
Zimbolicious: An Anthology of Zimbabwean Literature and Arts, Vol 3 by Tendai Mwanaka
Drawing Without Licence by Tendai R Mwanaka
Writing Grandmothers/ Escribiendo sobre nuestras raíces: Africa Vs Latin America Vol 2 by Tendai R Mwanaka and Felix Rodriguez

Nationalism: (Mis)Understanding Donald Trump's Capitalism, Racism, Global Politics, International Trade and Media Wars, Africa Vs North America Vol 2 by Tendai R Mwanaka

It Is Not About Me: Diaries 2010-2011 by Tendai Rinos Mwanaka

Chitungwiza Mushamukuru: An Anthology from Zimbabwe's Biggest Ghetto Town by Tendai Rinos Mwanaka

Soon to be released

Parks and Recreation by Abigail George
INFLUENCE OF CLIMATE VARIABILITY ON THE PREVALENCE OF DENGUE FEVER IN MANDERA COUNTY, KENYA by NDIWA JOSEPH KIMTAI
Writing Robotics, Africa Vs Asia, Vol 2 by Tendai Rinos Mwanaka

https://facebook.com/MwanakaMediaAndPublishing/

www.ingramcontent.com/pod-product-compliance
Lightning Source LLC
Chambersburg PA
CBHW051613230426
43668CB00013B/2085